So
You
Want
To
Grow
Spirituallly?

Ted Thwing

Table of Contents

Acknowledgements

I will always be deeply grateful to God for the opportunity to be around Bruce Larson when he was senior pastor at University Presbyterian Church in Seattle. He had a profound influence in shaping who I am as a Christian.

A special thanks to each of the two hundred people who took the time to be interviewed for the Spiritual Growth Project. Their stories and insight were stunning and fueled a large amount of the thinking from which this book was born.

I'm very grateful for the wonderful team of reviewers who have looked over various drafts of this book and provided helpful insight, feedback and suggestions that have greatly strengthened this book. These included Andi, Cathy, Courtney, Dave, David, Don, Erika, Hazel, James B., Jennifer, Jim, Laura, Lauren, Linda, Marcia, Mark, Martha, Peter, Phil, Renee, Rhonda, Steve, Summer and Tia.

Thanks to Abigail Platter for creating the illustrations used in Figures 3-2, 5-1, 10-3 and 10-4. Thanks to Jon Garcia, who provided Figure 10-1 and very helpful assistance with formatting all the illustrations. Thanks to Jay Flaming for the wonderful photographs used in Figures 4-3 and 9-2 and the intruder photo used in Figure 4-2.

I'm deeply grateful for all the wonderful work that Sue Lockett John has done as editor for this book project. Sue brought superb editorial expertise to the writing process, helping to guide and revise the writing. She was a very helpful critic, a wonderful encourager and a terrific coach. Sue showed a remarkable balance in working to improve the quality of the writing while still maintaining the voice of the author.

And finally, I deeply appreciate the work of all the people at The Editorial Department whose expertise and assistance prepared this book for publication.

Introduction

What are the key experiences that have shaped your life as a Christian? A pastor posed this question to me and a handful of other Christian leaders in preparation for an upcoming retreat. He was only looking for a page or two in response and it seemed like an interesting question, so I started writing. As I wrote, I sensed that taking this time to reflect on how God had been at work was a very valuable exercise. But when I finished, I was both puzzled and fascinated. The causes of my spiritual growth were not what we usually talk about in churches when we discuss Christian formation and discipleship. Was I just weird? Or is it possible that we are overlooking some significant causes of Christian spiritual growth?

I didn't do anything about these questions right away, but I kept thinking about them. Finally, a year later, I took my write-up with me on a long airplane trip so I could think about it some more. I became even more curious about the causes of spiritual growth, and I wondered what other people had experienced. So, on that flight, I planned out an interview project to ask other Christians what had caused their spiritual growth. Then I would be able to look at the interview results to determine the most significant causes of spiritual growth. Over the next fifteen months, I did two hundred such interviews (see Appendix A for a description of the process used for the interviews).

From these responses, I summarized some important actual causes of spiritual growth (see Appendix B). These results clearly show that there are indeed significant causes of spiritual growth that we are not talking about in churches. The interviews provided not only the data for evaluating the importance of factors that contribute to spiritual growth but also a rich tapestry of wisdom and insight about how these causes are woven into the experiences of life.

At first, I had no intention of writing a book. But after completing the interviews, I became convinced that the results were important, both for individual Christians and for our churches. So I set out to write a book in order to share what I had been learning from the interviews and from thinking about the cumulative results. Note that although the book does include some results from the interviews, it is not written as a full report on the project. Rather, it is written as the beginning of a discussion, to provoke thinking and discussion about spiritual growth.

In this book I have included a number of stories about real people to add depth and real-life examples for some of the key points. I am grateful for permission from these people to use their stories, though I have not used their real names. The one exception is the story of Ben Towne, whose parents have given me permission to include his name as well as the story about him.

I hope you will find this book thought-provoking and useful in thinking about your own spiritual growth and also about the spiritual growth of those who know you and those you lead.

Ted Thwing
Seattle, Washington

CHAPTER 1

Are You Related to God?

My wife and I were recently invited to spend an evening with a remarkable missionary couple who were doing amazing work with Muslim people in France and the Middle East. Although the host couple's home was only a short distance from ours, we did not know them. As we introduced ourselves and started getting acquainted, the host noted my last name and asked if I knew twin brothers with that same last name. He had gone to high school with these twins. With delight I grinned and told him I knew them very well; they were my two youngest brothers!

I've been thinking about that conversation. What if someone asked me if I were related to God? How would I respond? How *am* I related to God? How are you related to God? How would you answer that question?

And if you are related to God, how is it going? How long have you had this relationship? Are there times when it has grown more than others? And how is it now? Is that relationship growing or is it static, tired? Would you like it to grow? If you would like to grow in your relationship with God, I hope you find this book helpful and thought-provoking.

Are You Good Enough?

Let's try an introductory exercise using Figure 1-1 below:

- Where would you put yourself on the line between 100% bad and 100% good? Put an X there.
- Can you think of a person you would judge to be farther to the right on the line? Put an A at that point.
- Can you think of a person who might be farther to the left on the line? Put a B at that point.
- Where do you think other people see you on the line? Put an O there.
- Where do you think God sees you? Put a G there.

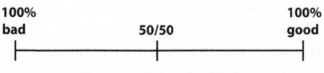

Figure 1-1. Bad-to-Good Scale

The amazing news of the Gospel is that God accepts us right where we are. Wherever you put the X on the line in the figure above, God accepts you there. And then he grows you from where you are. In this life, we never get to 100% good—not even close. As the apostle Paul wrote in his letter to the church at Rome, "All have sinned and fall short of the glory of God."[1] I think he could have said "far short." And remember, he was writing to Christians! Bruce Larson, a former senior pastor of University Presbyterian Church in Seattle, said it pointedly in the title of a wonderful article in *Leadership Journal*: "None of Us Are Sinner Emeritus."[2] We have not graduated from the human race.

Paul wrote to the church at Ephesus that "it is by grace you have been saved, through faith—and this not from yourselves, it is the gift of God—not by works, so that no one can boast."[3] So are all of us accepted, no matter where we are on the line? Yes. We are saved by grace, not by how good we are. Jesus has taken care of the rest of the line. We can't reach it on our own.

What does this mean for us? It means that God knows us completely *and* he loves us completely. I had the delightful opportunity one evening to talk to a rather large group of people who worked with children in a church. My introductory comments included these words:

> *The creator of the universe knows who I am. He even knows my name. In fact, he knows the right-down-to-the-core-who-I-really-am me. And he loves me. This love is so basic that even a young child can begin to understand it. And yet it is so high and wide and deep that no matter how long I live, I will never fully understand it or comprehend it. Sometimes it just seems too good to be true. But it is true; Jesus loves me and Jesus loves you.*

Since God meets us where we really are and loves us where we really are and grows us from where we really are, we all have amazing opportunities to grow. No matter where we are today (or how old we are), our relationship with God can grow. Doesn't that sound like good news?

The Problem of Spiritual Maturity

Some people like to talk about spiritual maturity. I don't and I
wish they didn't. At first it seems to make so much sense. Why
shouldn't we expect to grow spiritually? Why shouldn't we expect
to get better and better? And if we do, doesn't it make sense that
we might improve so much that our growth slows down? Might
a person run out of room to grow much more?

Figure 1-2 pictures what many people think about spiritual maturity. According to this thinking, when you start out
in life, you aren't especially aware of what's going on spiritually,
so there's not much spiritual growth. At some point, you start
to understand a bit about life and God and you begin to grow
toward spiritual maturity. You have various periods of growth,
and over time you understand more and more. Eventually you
become spiritually mature. You have learned a lot, and other
people recognize that and look to you for advice.

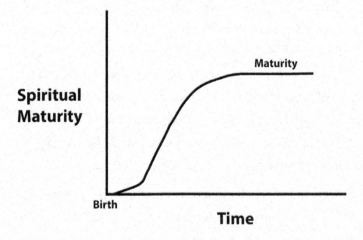

Figure 1-2. Spiritual Maturity

I believe this spiritual maturity model is unhealthy for several reasons:

- We never run out of room to grow spiritually. There is always more (probably much more) that God can teach us, no matter how long we live. We do acquire more knowledge, yes. We do learn from having more experiences, yes. But God has so much to teach us that we still don't understand, no matter how long we have been Christians.
- We don't "arrive" at spiritual maturity. Not in this life. It's unhealthy to think we've reached a level where we no longer need to grow. People who think they have arrived don't understand their situation and are not healthy models. On the contrary, this attitude shows a stagnant relationship with God and a deep need for a spurt of spiritual growth.
- Finally, it's not how much we know or how much we have experienced that determines our spiritual vitality; it's how much we are growing. So if we sense we have arrived, we are not growing and we are much in need of some spiritual growth to regain spiritual vitality.

Figure 1-3 has the same spiritual maturity curve as Figure 1-2, but I've added a graph below it to show how much spiritual growth is occurring during each part of the spiritual maturity curve above it. In other words, the bottom graph is a measure of spiritual vitality. It shows the problem with the thinking behind the spiritual maturity curve. Early on, there may not be much spiritual growth. That's fine. Then there is a wonderful period of high spiritual growth. That's fine too.

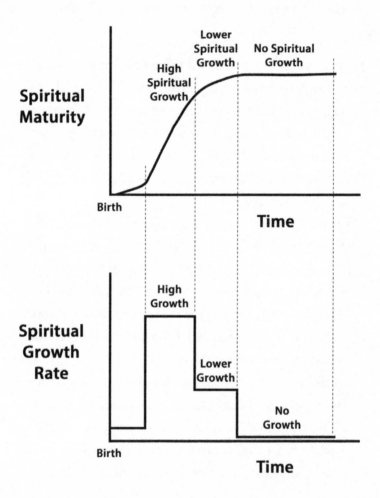

Figure 1-3. Spiritual Growth Rates

Then follows a period of lower spiritual growth. That's not unusual; no one goes through life at a sustained high level of growth. Then there is a time of no spiritual growth. That's not unusual either. But it is unhealthy to never again have a period of spiritual growth.

Our spiritual vitality is not related to how much we know or understand or even how much we have experienced; instead, it is related to how much we are growing. We grow more at some periods of life than at others. And we decline at times. But we are the most healthy in our relationship with God when we are growing. So we need these growth times. And to be our healthiest, we need these times of growing to be spread across our lifetime. But what causes this growth?

The Spiritual Growth Research Project

The Spiritual Growth Research Project (SG Project) was designed to investigate this question of what causes spiritual growth. Interviews were conducted with two hundred people in the Seattle area. Interviewees were invited to reflect on their lives from birth to present, divide them into a number of periods and think about how much spiritual growth they experienced in each period. Then interviewees were invited to put this information in a graph that showed how much spiritual growth they believed they experienced in each period (Figure 1.4 shows an example of one such life graph). The interview then explored what had caused the spiritual growth in each of the higher-growth periods. A summary of the research process is shown in Appendix A, and a summary of interview results is included in Appendix B.

From an analysis of all the life graphs obtained in the interviews, the SG Project found the following key characteristics of spiritual growth:

- Spiritual growth occurs at many different levels across a lifetime. Some periods can be high-growth,

some can be low-growth, some can be zero-growth
and some can be periods of spiritual decline.

- Spiritual growth seems never to be constantly high;
  you can't plan on always growing at a significant
  level. Life just isn't like that.
- Spiritual growth can occur at almost any time in life.
- There is no typical graph for spiritual growth across a
  lifetime. The spiritual growth graphs for each person
  were almost as unique as fingerprints.

Figure 1-4 is an example of a life graph obtained from one of
the interviews. It shows that this person was aware of beginning
spiritual growth at a very young age. There was significant growth
in high school and college, followed by mostly low growth from
ages twenty-three to forty-seven. Finally, there was significant
growth from ages forty-eight to sixty-two, the age at which the
interview was conducted. This person experienced the highest
spiritual growth after age fifty-six.

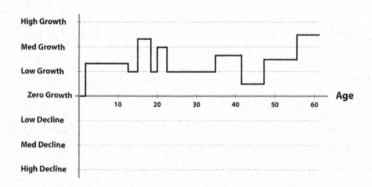

Figure 1-4. Example 1 of Real-Life Spiritual Growth

As a second example of significant growth in later years, Figure 1-5 shows the life graph of a person who was aware of a bit

of very early spiritual growth, a period of decline in the twen-
ties, then significant growth from ages thirty-six to forty-two
and again after age seventy. This person experienced the highest
spiritual growth after age seventy-five.

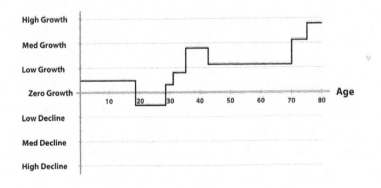

Figure 1-5. Example 2 of Real-Life Spiritual Growth

These two examples are not necessarily representative of
everyone sixty or older, but both graphs show that significant
spiritual growth can occur after the age of sixty. In fact, of the
thirty-four people interviewed who were sixty-five or over,
twenty-eight (82%) reported significant spiritual growth after
the age of sixty. These results suggest that it's never too late to
grow spiritually and that we never run out of room to grow.

Spiritual Decline

Although the SG Project focused on the causes of spiritual
growth, the interviews also gave some insight into spiritual stag-
nation or decline. The results show that a drop from a significant
level of spiritual growth can occur at any period of life, no matter

how long a person has been a Christian. The most frequently observed causes of such a drop were the following:

- A post-college period when young people are trying to figure out who they are now that they are on their own
- Leaving the nest of supportive community
- Finding it difficult to get connected to Christian friends after a move
- Encountering tough times
- Distractions due to life pressures that come from starting a family
- Distractions from life pressures related to work
- Lack of challenge (when a period of life is easy)

Getting Started

Maybe you started reading this book because you are feeling a need or desire to grow spiritually or to experience more spiritual vitality. If so, I hope you find that you have come to the right place. The rest of this book is all about some key causes of spiritual growth and incorporates the insights of two hundred people about what caused them to grow. I hope that one or more of these causes will resonate with you. I also hope that this book leads you to encounter the work of God from the inside out. Spiritual growth is an inside job.

You might consider starting by doing the exercises used in the SG Project yourself. To do so, use the two interview pages and explanations shown in Appendix A.

I also invite you to pray and ask God for help in growing

spiritually. You could use the short prayer that follows or, if you prefer, create one like it in your own words:

> *God, I'd really like to grow spiritually,*
>
> *not just to know more or experience more,*
>
> *but to have a more vital, meaningful relationship with you.*
>
> *Would you please help me?*

I know of few prayers that God is more likely to answer in a wonderful way!

CHAPTER 2

Tough Times

Have you experienced significant tough times in life? Or has life been rather easy for you? Have tough times in your life led to spiritual growth or to spiritual decline? Have you grown spiritually more in the tough times of your life or in the easy times?

For sure, tough experiences don't always lead to spiritual growth; sometimes they cause spiritual decline. But in some amazing ways, God can bring significant spiritual growth out of tough times. It was interesting to discover from the SG Project that the most frequently noted cause of high spiritual growth was "tough times" (see Figure B-2 in Appendix B). Sometimes this growth springs right out of the middle of a tough time in life. At other times it's a delayed reaction, becoming apparent only later. In any case, it can encourage us during a hard period of life to know that God can use even the really tough stuff for a good purpose.

God Can Bring Good from Tough Times

In Paul's letter to Christians in Rome, he makes a statement about tough times that is often misunderstood:

> *And we know that in all things God works for the good of those who love him…*[1]

Note that Paul is not saying that all things that happen in life are good; he is saying that God can bring good out of even the tough events in life. It's not that God sends the tough times, but he can use even those unwelcome events to bring good in our lives.

A few years ago, Ben, a friend's two-year old son, was diagnosed with neuroblastoma, an aggressive form of cancer. As you can imagine, this horrible news was a huge shock to Ben's parents and utterly devastating to them. The very experienced members of Ben's medical team tried every treatment they knew to fight the cancer (chemotherapy, radiation, a stem cell transplant, antibody therapies and surgery), but after a brave sixteen-month fight, Ben lost his battle with neuroblastoma and died.

Words cannot describe the agony and pain that Ben suffered as the cancer ravaged his small body and as he endured the difficult side effects of his treatments. Words cannot describe his parents' agony and pain at seeing their young son, whom they deeply loved, suffer so terribly. And words cannot describe the agony and pain his parents experienced when they finally lost their son in death.

Out of their grief in losing Ben to cancer, his parents came up with the idea of creating a foundation to support pediatric

cancer research. Their foundation has been remarkably successful in raising funds to support research to find new ways to treat
cancer in children. It is already clear that this research is making very important progress toward completely new methods of
treatment. The objective is to "provide a new standard of care
for childhood cancer—one where a child's own blood becomes
the source for the cure. There's no surgery, no chemotherapy, no
radiation and the worst side effects are having symptoms of a
common cold for a few days."[2]

Was Ben's cancer a good thing? Certainly not! Did God send
this cancer to Ben? What a grotesque thought! But God is using
Ben's parents and their indescribable pain and agony to bring
great good for the treatment of other children.

In the book of Genesis, we read another story about how God
can use a bad situation to bring good. This story is about Joseph,
who was severely mistreated by his brothers, who hated him.
They talked about killing him, but instead they tossed him into
a pit and later sold him to a passing caravan on its way to Egypt.
Joseph had many tough experiences in Egypt, but God was with
him. Eventually he rose to a powerful position in the court of the
Egyptian Pharaoh and saved the country from starvation. Then,
through some remarkable events, Joseph and his brothers were
reconciled. But the brothers never forgot that they had treated
Joseph so badly. Years later, when their father, Jacob, died, they
were very anxious that Joseph might now take his revenge. So
the brothers came to Joseph in abject fear and humility. Here is
how the book of Genesis describes this encounter:

> *His brothers then came and threw themselves down
> before him. "We are your slaves," they said.*

But Joseph said to them, "Don't be afraid. Am I in the
place of God? You intended to harm me, but God intended
it for good to accomplish what is now being done, the sav-
ing of many lives. So then, don't be afraid. I will provide
for you and your children." And he reassured them and
spoke kindly to them.[3]

What had happened to Joseph at the hands of his brothers was certainly not good. But Joseph had a remarkable understanding that in spite of the harmful intentions of his brothers,
God had used even those difficult circumstances for good.

In the New Testament, the death of Jesus is another example
of how God can take the worst stuff encountered in life and use it
for great good. Out of his great love for people, God sent his only
son to earth with good news about the possibility of reconciliation
with him, but people refused to listen and they killed him. This is
not by any means a good thing; it is the greatest evil people could
have done. Yet God used that almost-unthinkable evil to bring
about the greatest possible good—to provide the means for us to
have our sins forgiven and to receive God's offer of a grace-filled
relationship with him. It also gives us confidence that God understands suffering, loss and pain. Jesus came into our world and lived
in the midst of its suffering; he experienced it himself.

For another example, look at how God brought good out of
the tough times surrounding persecution of the early Church in
Jerusalem. After the death and resurrection of Jesus, the religious
authorities in Jerusalem were very concerned about the rapidly
growing number of people who were following Jesus. The early
apostles were arrested and placed in jail. Stephen was put on trial
and then stoned to death. After Stephen's death, a great persecution broke out against Christians, and as a result, many left

Jerusalem and scattered across Judea and Samaria.[4] Some moved to even more distant places, such as Damascus, Phoenicia, Cyprus and Antioch. Persecution caused some really tough times for the early Christians in Jerusalem, but God used it in important ways to expand Christianity beyond Jerusalem to other nearby and distant towns.

The amazing news is that God can use the tough periods in our lives to help us grow spiritually. Tough times can remind us that we need God and motivate us to turn to him in a deeper way. As one of those interviewed for the SG Project observed:

> *When life is easy and we're having fun, I don't think we tend to grow spiritually. But we grow in tough times.*

Another interviewee said:

> *A lot of my spiritual growth has to do with crises in my life.*

Nonetheless, growth from tough times still involves a lot of pain. One person recalled a particularly tough stretch of life with these words:

> *This was a period of a huge amount of growth, but in a really painful way (these two things are close together).*

And another put it this way:

> *I hate the tough times; sometimes I like the result.*

Interestingly, even though tough times were identified as one of the major causes of spiritual growth, this growth wasn't always clear at the time; sometimes awareness came in retrospect. As one of the interviewees noted:

> *Growing in the midst of tough times? In the moment, no. I was just in there hanging on. But later, because of that, yes.*

Tough Times Are Part of Life

Nobody enjoys the tough times in life, but everyone has them. As Lucy says in the Peanuts comic strip in Figure 2-1, we don't want downs in our life; we just want ups and ups and ups. But tough times do occur in the course of life. As one interviewee in the SG Project put it:

> *Going through tough times is just life.*

Another person said that no one chooses tough times, but they still occur:

> *You never elect this one; it just happens.*

Figure 2-1. Lucy Wants Only Ups

For sure, some people experience much tougher times than others, and tough times come in a variety of flavors. The SG

Project identified five causes of tough times. Some come from our own bad choices. If I rob a bank and wind up in prison, the tough times I encounter are the result of a bad choice I made. The same was true in the parable of the prodigal son, found in the Bible in the book of Luke.[5] The hard times the son faced after leaving home and squandering his inheritance were simply the result of his bad life choices.

Other tough times result from other people's bad choices. I might suffer tough times if a drunk driver crosses over into my lane and smashes into my car. Or maybe I'm caught up in a war when my country is invaded. Or maybe my retirement savings evaporate because some unscrupulous person has made off with my money. All these tough times are the result of bad choices someone else has made, but they directly affect me.

We can also encounter tough times simply because we live in a world that is at odds with God's original design. Our fallen world has anopheles mosquitoes in some places, and I can get malaria from being bitten by one. Or I can get cancer; it just happens. No one makes choices that cause these tough times, but they occur because we live in a fallen world.

I can also face tough times when something important to me is not important to another person. Maybe I really like spending time with a particular woman, but eventually she decides that she is interested in someone else. This results in a very tough time for me; it hurts. Or maybe my company is bought by another one and my job is no longer needed, so I get laid off. I might experience a tough time while looking for another job.

We also can experience tough times when we choose to come alongside people who are hurting. As we care for them in their suffering, we experience part of their pain in a way that can be tough for us as well. It's deeply meaningful to realize that this is what God did when he chose to enter our hurting world and come alongside us. This is the amazing news of the incarnation that we celebrate at Christmas.

Dealing with Tough Times

Inevitably, we encounter tough experiences in life. What happens when we encounter these? How do we deal with them? One way is shown in Figure 2-2. Suppose we run into a problem big enough that we realize we need help in dealing with it and eventually decide to turn to God for help. God can intervene and help us through the problem, and then life can become OK again.

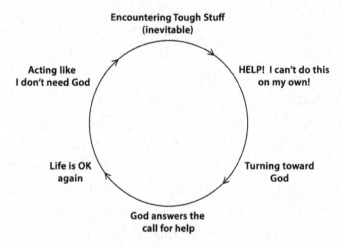

Figure 2-2. One Possible Cycle of Tough Times

But when life becomes comfortable again, it's easy to forget God and his healing power. We may then fall into the rut of living and acting as if we don't need God any longer (at least until the next crisis). As one interviewee commented about a comfortable period in his life:

> *This was a great period and a great experience because it was relatively easy. I was having all kinds of fun and thinking I've got this pretty well wired.*

This person did not feel the need for God in this easy period of life when he was confident that he could do it on his own, without God. It is worth noting that he evaluated this period as a time of low spiritual growth.

Of course, some tough times in life do not have quick resolutions. Instead of completing the cycle in Figure 2-2, life does not quickly become OK again. We realize that this tough period of life is more than we can handle on our own and turn to God for help—we pour our hearts out to him—but we don't see any answer in response. As illustrated in Figure 2-3, we feel stuck in the cycle, waiting for God to respond to our heartfelt cries for help. We can begin to wonder where God is. When we are stuck in a tough period of life like this, we may not grow spiritually; in fact, we might experience spiritual decline.

Figure 2-3. Stuck!

Hopefully, in times like this, we eventually realize that the approach to life suggested by Figure 2-3 is not adequate to handle the toughest times we might face. This view of life and God's role in it is inadequate in two important ways: it won't help us through the most difficult stretches in life, and such a view of God and his role in our life is far too limited. Basically, it views God only as "Mr. Fix-It," there to fix the problems we encounter so we can move on to a place where we don't need him any longer.

Fortunately, God is much bigger than this limited view, and his role in our lives can be much bigger as well. There is a deeper, more meaningful way to go through tough times, and it leads to much more spiritual growth. Figure 2-4 shows the same encounter with tough times but with important differences. First, we more quickly turn to God for help. And in the middle of the tough time, we choose to trust God and to share our lives (things we enjoy and things we find hard) with him. We listen for God in our lives and learn about his presence in our lives even in the midst of the tough stuff. We learn to look for the things in life for which we can be grateful even as we experience pain and suffering. And we thank God for these blessings even as we share our anguish over the things that hurt. As we see God's hand helping us through the tough times (often working through other people), we thank him for his presence in our lives and for coming alongside in the midst of the tough stuff we experience. After the tough stuff resolves, we listen to God for the next steps, and when the time is right, we are able to explore and risk those next steps. But, of course, there are always more crises in life in which we go through new cycles of learning to trust God and looking for him at work in our lives.

Figure 2-4. Cycle with a Deeper Relationship with God

Tough Times Can Result in Spiritual Growth

While no one likes the tough times in life, we can often see that valuable things come out of them. In his letter to the Christians in Rome, Paul included this remarkable statement about the value of the sufferings he had encountered:

> *And not only that, but we also boast in our sufferings, knowing that suffering produces endurance, and endurance produces character, and character produces hope, and hope does not disappoint us, because God's love has been poured into our hearts through the Holy Spirit that has been given to us. (NRSV)*[6]

Like Paul, many other Christians have discovered that God can use even the tough times in life for good, and we can use tough times to grow spiritually.

One of the people interviewed for the SG Project noted that tough times and the spiritual good that can come from them are much like what happens as a result of physical exercise. After vigorous exercise, we often feel significant muscle soreness. It hurts. The cause of this soreness is fascinating. When our muscles are asked to work harder than usual, they suffer from what are called micro-tears. The natural healing processes that repair these tiny tears cause inflammation and swelling in the days following the extra physical activity. But it turns out that these tiny muscle tears are part of the normal process of growth in the body; they're *necessary* for muscle growth. The tears happen at the places where muscles cannot handle the stresses they encounter, and they cause growth exactly where needed. The resulting soreness is part of a process that helps us build muscles and improve strength and power.

Are you facing tough times? Or do you know someone who is experiencing a tough stretch of life? If so, I invite you to consider asking God for his powerful presence in the middle of these tough times to somehow bring good out of times that are definitely not good in themselves. You could use the following prayer or, if you prefer, create one like it in your own words:

> *Dear God,*
>
> *Thank you for your wonderful love for our world that caused you to send your son Jesus into the middle of this world with so much tough stuff in it.*
>
> *Thanks for sending Jesus into the middle of my world. It's amazing news that you know me, understand what I'm going through and love me deeply no matter what is going on in my life.*
>
> *You know the tough challenges I'm facing in my life; you*

know where life is not easy for me and where it hurts.

In the middle of these tough times, I ask for your reassurance that you know me, that you understand what I'm going through and that you love me deeply.

And most particularly, I ask for your powerful redeeming presence in these tough times in my life. Please use these times as only you can to help me grow in my relationship with you and to care more deeply about other people who are experiencing tough stuff.

Please open my eyes to see your presence in my life and to trust you, especially in the midst of the tough times in life.

CHAPTER 3

Trusting God

Spiritual growth from trusting God is not usually associated with the comfortable and easy. As we saw in the previous chapter, spiritual growth can occur when we encounter hard times in life. It also can happen when we are faced with important choices, when we take an important risk to do something for God and when a new challenge stretches us. In these life situations, we realize much more clearly that we depend on God and that we have a strong need to trust him. The results of the SG Project indicate that trusting God is one of the top causes of spiritual growth (see Appendix B).

How Much Do We Need God?

Although I don't want to live this way, I find that I can easily go through a day and not really be conscious of God's role in my life or in the world around me. I often seem to have a lot of control over what happens in my day. I can wake up in the morning and make a plan for the day, and the day often unfolds about the way I have it pictured. Though I wouldn't ever say this to God, I realize that leaving God out of planning for my day in effect tells him, "I think I've got this day under control. I don't think I'll be needing you, but if I do, I'll yell."

Being independent is very important to Americans. Our nation started with a declaration of independence. The spirit of independence continued to grow on the American frontier, where people did not have others around them and they had to make it on their own. Even now, more than two hundred years after the birth of our country, this determination to be independent, to make it on our own, continues to be a strong part of the American culture. We consider ourselves resourceful. Our first reaction is to try to make it on our own, and this makes it hard to ask for help even when we realize we need it.

Of course, we are not really independent, and we do need people around us. We become particularly aware of our need for other people when we hit the tough patches of life. In those times we also become aware—or are reminded—of how important it is to be able to look to God for help.

My awareness of how much I need God depends very much on how I view my current situation and how on top of it I feel. Think about the five situations below that I might experience; they are arranged in order of increasing difficulty:

1. I have a plan for this situation, and I'm confident my plan will work.
2. I don't have a plan for this situation, but I'm

confident I can come up with something that will work out.

3. I don't have a plan for this situation, and I hope I can find someone who can help solve the problem.

4. I don't have a plan for this situation, and I'm not sure I will be able to find one that will work.

5. I don't have a plan, and I think the situation is too difficult for anyone to have a plan.

In Figure 3-1, I've placed these five situations in a chart to illustrate the degree to which they drive me to think that I need to trust God for a solution. For situations 1 and 2, I'm confident that I'll do OK on my own, and I don't need help from anyone else. For situation 3, I realize I may need some help, and I'm looking for people who might be able to help. In situation 4, I'm thinking the situation is difficult enough that I might not be able to find anyone who can help, and I'm starting to think I might need God's intervention. In situation 5, I know God is my only hope.

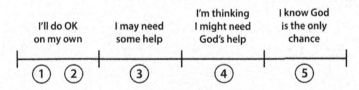

Figure 3-1. Spectrum of Trusting God

The SG Project results (Appendix B) show that needing to trust God because I'm in over my head is one of the top five causes of spiritual growth. When in over my head, I know I need to trust God, and I grow in my ability to do that. In a letter to the church at Corinth, Paul said it this way:

We do not want you to be uninformed, brothers and sisters, about the troubles we experienced in the province of Asia. We were under great pressure, far beyond our ability to endure, so that we despaired of life itself. Indeed, we felt we had received the sentence of death. But this happened that we might not rely on ourselves but on God, who raises the dead. [1]

When we get to the end of our rope, we realize that it isn't enough to trust in ourselves; we need to put our trust in God. He is the only one who can provide a solution when we are in way over our heads. One person interviewed in the SG Project said this about a period of high spiritual growth in which he had lost two different jobs:

I was in over my head. My spiritual growth is when I'm in over my head and I need God. I never gave up that God had something for me. I was changing my direction real fast.

Another person recalled:

I was on a mission team to Haiti the summer Haiti had a big earthquake. I was stretched in places where I did not yet have any skills. I sensed God saying to me, "No, you need me in all of this." Intellectually, I knew this before. But I'm realizing that everything I'm good at isn't working. I thought I could do it, but it didn't work without God. I spent a lot of time praying about the situation.

When rating the impact on spiritual growth of "needing to trust God because I'm in over my head," another person noted:

> *Sometimes you recognize in advance that you're going to be over your head. But other times, once you get into it, you uncover things that emerge.*

In other words, unexpected events in our lives can cause spiritual growth.

One interviewee, Tim, described a remarkable afternoon at work during which he was definitely aware of being in over his head and needing to trust God. One of his co-workers came running into his second-floor office saying that another co-worker was outside in the parking lot shooting at the windows of the building. The shooter was wearing fatigues and, in addition to the rifle in his hands, had a knife in his belt.

As the other people in the building quickly evacuated, Tim called 911. After a short amount of time, the shooter entered the building, and the 911 operator told Tim not to leave his office because it would be too dangerous. He was instructed to lock his office door and climb under his enclosed desk. Tim remained on the phone talking with the operator. Soon a police detective came on the line and started asking questions to keep up with what was going on in the building. Meanwhile, the gunman, who knew the building systems, walked by the receptionist's console and saw a light indicating that a phone in the building was in use. He could see that it was Tim's phone line, and he headed to Tim's office.

By this time a SWAT team had assembled behind a grass ridge at the edge of the parking lot while a news helicopter circled overhead. The gunman quickly reached Tim's office, knocked on the locked door and yelled, "Tim, I want you to leave the building!" Tim got out from under his desk, opened the door and held up the phone in his hand. "There are people on the phone who can help you," Tim said. He didn't really feel threatened, but he sure was scared; he felt his heart pounding in his chest. The gunman came into the office and they had something of a conversation, but he was clearly upset and not rational. He would listen for a bit and then go off on an emotional rant.

Eventually the detective, who had been listening to the conversation on the phone, told Tim to go downstairs to the receptionist's console to connect an additional outside line to Tim's phone to enable a good friend of the gunman to talk to him. The detective then wanted Tim to escape out the front door.

Tim started to go downstairs, but as soon as he walked out of his office, he had a strong sense from the Holy Spirit that he should not seek safety by leaving the building but instead return to his office to be with the gunman. So after going downstairs to the receptionist's console, he came back to his office. The gunman was surprised to see Tim return, and it became easier to have a conversation. At one point the gunman told Tim, "I'm worth nothing." To which Tim replied with a phrase he had heard: "No, no. God don't make no junk." (Later, the gunman told Tim that this had been a turning point for him.)

The gunman then left the office and did some damage to a nearby room, but he came back and threw his rifle and knife through the glass of Tim's office window, followed by his bullets. The detective, who had continued to monitor their conversation on the phone, now instructed Tim that he and the gunman were to go downstairs and come out the front door with their hands on their heads. The gunman agreed to do this. As they came out the front door, the SWAT team ordered both of them to lie flat on the ground and handcuffed them both (as a precaution in case the gunman had exchanged clothes with Tim). At that point, a building manager identified Tim and the gunman, and the tense ordeal came to an end.

Tim summed up this very formative experience with these words:

> It was a traumatic time but also a time of tremendous reassurance. I knew God's presence in a very real way. I had a strong sense of the presence of God and that I could trust him in the midst of this danger.

Another interviewee in the SG Project succinctly summed up the impact on spiritual growth that comes from trusting God when in over our heads with this comment:

> If you don't give the highest rating to 'trusting God when I'm in over my head,' you haven't been there.

The results of the SG Project suggest several situations that cause us to trust God when we are in over our heads: going through tough times, choosing to obey God's nudge/call/invitation and taking a risk. As we discovered in the previous chapter, going through tough times can lead us to trust God and, as a result, to grow spiritually. Choosing to obey God's nudge/call/invitation, as Tim did, is likely to lead us into situations where we need to trust God and, in doing so, we grow spiritually. Choosing to take a risk to follow God also is likely to lead us into situations where we need to trust God, and here, too, we experience spiritual growth.

Choosing to Trust God

Trusting God is always a choice. We can choose to trust God or not. Of course, it's easier to choose to trust ourselves rather than God when life is easy. And we're more likely to choose to trust God when we are in over our heads. Trusting God comes down to life choices we make. It's more than just what we know, think or believe is true. I like the way Bruce Larson said it:

> You see, God asks us ... questions when we try to get close to him. They are not true-or-false questions; they are yes-or-no. Lots of people say "True" to the Atonement, the Resurrection, the Second Coming, but that's like saying, "True, I believe in marriage." Not until you say "Yes" to a person are you actually married.
>
> So God's first question to you is not "Do you believe in the concept of discipleship?" It is rather this: "Will you trust me with your life, yes or no?" That's what he said to Abram (later called Abraham): "Will you leave the familiar, sell your house, pack up your goods, and move out?"[2]

Choosing to trust God can be hard to do because we are often aware that we need to let go of something in order to pursue the new possibility. Larson often talked about a trapeze to describe this transition (see Figure 3-2).

Illustration by Abigail Platter

Figure 3-2. Trusting God for the Next Step

To move from one trapeze to the next, the trapeze artist must let go of one trapeze before grasping the next. Like the trapeze artist, we may be comfortable in our current situation. But to pursue the new possibility, we have to let go of the old, the familiar. In the in-between period, we are very aware of the need to trust God. It is a great opportunity to grow spiritually.

Sometimes trusting God involves trusting that he knows what he is doing. In Luke 5 we read a remarkable fishing story.[3] Peter the fisherman and his partners, James and John, were very experienced in fishing and in catching fish; it was their livelihood.

But one day Jesus walked by while they were washing their nets after having caught nothing the night before. He asked Peter to row him out a bit into the lake where Jesus could sit in the boat and teach the people gathered on the shore. After Jesus finished teaching, he gave Peter some odd instructions about fishing. He told Peter to go back out to the deep water and let his nets down for a catch. But it was the wrong time of day to fish; it was the time for cleaning the nets, not fishing. Furthermore, Peter and his partners had not been successful fishing in that area the night before. And it's also worth noting that this was a carpenter giving the fishermen advice on how to fish! But after objecting, Peter, James and John did as Jesus asked. The result was astonishing. They caught so many fish that their nets began to break. They had their partners in a nearby boat come to help, and they filled both boats so full of fish that they began to sink.

It was remarkable to catch so many fish, but what happened next was even more remarkable. Jesus invited the fishermen to trust him even further. He invited them to follow him and he would make them fishers of people. Of course, these men knew how to fish for fish, but they couldn't have had a clue about how to fish for people. In following Jesus, they had to trust that he could teach them to "fish" for people. They trusted that Jesus knew what he was doing, and they chose to follow him.

Sometimes trusting God involves following his invitation to do what seems impossible. In Matthew 14 there is an account of a dark and stormy night when the disciples were attempting to cross the Sea of Galilee in a boat to get back home. Jesus had stayed behind on the far side of the lake and sent them on ahead. It was the middle of the night, and the boat was buffeted by the waves because the wind was against them. This was a scene that could terrify grown men, especially experienced fishermen who knew that the storms on the Sea of Galilee could be very dangerous. But what really frightened the disciples in the middle of the storm was seeing a man walking toward them across the top of the water. It was Jesus, but they didn't know that. Thinking it was a ghost, they were terrified. This is how Matthew describes what happened next:

> *But Jesus immediately said to them: "Take courage! It is I. Don't be afraid."*
>
> *"Lord, if it's you," Peter replied, "tell me to come to you on the water."*
>
> *"Come," he said.*
>
> *Then Peter got down out of the boat, walked on the water and came toward Jesus. But when he saw the wind, he was afraid and, beginning to sink, cried out, "Lord, save me!"*
>
> *Immediately Jesus reached out his hand and caught him. "You of little faith," he said, "why did you doubt?"*
>
> *And when they climbed into the boat, the wind died down. Then those who were in the boat worshiped him, saying, "Truly you are the Son of God."[4]*

This is a remarkable account. Peter did choose to trust Jesus enough to get out of the boat, but when he realized the situation he had gotten himself into, he was terrified. Could he really trust Jesus in the middle of *this*? His reaction was to cry out to Jesus for help, and Jesus reached out his hand and caught him. Jesus had asked Peter a very important question: "Why did you doubt?" Clearly, Jesus was much bigger than Peter and the rest of the disciples could even imagine! They had seen enough to realize that Jesus was truly the Son of God, and they worshipped him. They also were astonished at the degree to which he could be trusted.

Forks in the Road

Sometimes trusting God involves leaving what we know and what is familiar. In the book of Ruth there is a remarkable story of Ruth, who chose to leave her familiar surroundings in the country of Moab.[5] The story starts with a woman named Naomi who lived with her husband and two sons in Bethlehem, in the land of Judah. When a serious famine developed in Judah, Naomi and her family moved to Moab to live for a while. While there, Naomi's husband died, and she was left with just her two sons. Fortunately, her sons had married two wonderful Moabite women, Ruth and Orpah, who cared not only for the sons but now also for Naomi. After about ten years, the two sons also died, leaving Naomi with no immediate family.

Though Naomi had a close relationship with her daughters-in-law, when she received word that the famine in Judah was over, she decided to return to her homeland. She urged Ruth and Orpah to return to their families in Moab rather than leave their familiar surroundings, their relatives and their country. After much anguish, Orpah finally agreed to stay in Moab, but Ruth insisted on going with Naomi to Judah. This is what Ruth told Naomi:

> Don't urge me to leave you or to turn back from you. Where you go I will go, and where you stay I will stay. Your people will be my people and your God my God.[6]

Ruth left her familiar life in Moab to follow Naomi into a completely different adventure. Ruth had no way of knowing this choice would lead to her marriage to a wonderful man in Judah. And she certainly could not have imagined that a few generations later, one of her descendants would be the most important king in Israel's history.

I remember an important conversation with my dad about key decisions he had made in his life. As a framework for this conversation, my daughter and I had put together a list of questions we wanted to ask. One of my nieces acted as interviewer, and my dad responded to each of the questions. I recorded the whole interaction. It was a deeply meaningful experience and a wonderful way to learn about what was important to my dad and what had gone through his mind in each of these decisions. As we talked about these key experiences, we referred to them as "forks in the road."

As shown in Figure 3-3, key choices in life (forks in the road) can take a number of different forms. Sometimes on the road of life, we face opportunities to choose between branches that naturally continue from the road we are already on. Such a fork in the road might be choosing where to go for college. Maybe it's what job offer to accept or deciding where to live. At other times in life, a key choice might take a more abrupt form, where our current road just ends and we need to decide what to do now. Maybe a job ends. Maybe someone important to us dies. Maybe a key friend moves to another town far away. A third form of key choice in life comes when we choose to leave the life road we are on, like taking an exit from the freeway. Instead of just continuing along a familiar course, we decide to make a change, to take a risk to move in a different direction. We do this because we sense the road we are on is not taking us in the direction we want to be going. All these key choices, whatever the form, shape our life in important ways.

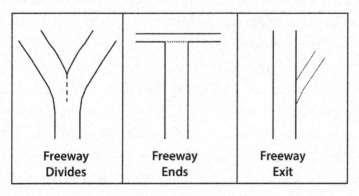

Figure 3-3. Choices

What have been the significant forks in your road? You might find it valuable to draw a map of your life identifying the key choices you have made. Were some of these choices natural continuations of the path you were on? Were some of these choices caused by an abrupt end to the road you were traveling? Were some of the choices an exit from the freeway, choices you made to significantly change the direction in which you were headed?

Some choices in life are difficult because there doesn't seem to be an obviously "right" choice among the available alternatives. You want to make a choice that best fits how God has designed you, but you are not sure what that choice should be. In these choices it is wonderful to know that God understands us completely and that we live in grace. So we can go forward making the best choice we can, and we can trust God with that choice.

Our key choices in life are wonderful opportunities for God to help us grow spiritually as we trust in him. God can even use choices that prove to be mistakes. As Bruce Larson often suggested, God may be able to use our mistakes even more than what we see as our successes. Our mistakes make us realize that we can't do it on our own, that we do need to trust God and do it his way, that we do need his intervention in our lives to pull off what we try to do for him.

In his second letter to the church at Corinth, Paul made a similar point.[7] He came to realize that God's grace was wide enough and deep enough to make his power especially evident at Paul's points of weakness. When we are weak, we are more aware of our need to depend on God's power at work through us. And this draws us to trust God rather than ourselves. Thus, like Paul, we can conclude that when we are weak, then we are strong.

When Larson talked with people about making key life choices, he often advised them to choose the riskier alternative that was available. I suspect this was because he knew that the riskier choice would make us more likely to be in over our heads and more highly motivated to trust God because we know we must.

Henrietta Mears made an amazing impact for God while serving for many years as director of Christian education at Hollywood Presbyterian Church. God used her in remarkable ways to influence people such as Billy Graham, Bill and Vonette Bright, Richard Halverson, Louis Evans Jr., Earl Palmer and many others who later became key leaders in the church. Billy Graham has said Henrietta Mears "was certainly one of the greatest Christians I have ever known!"[8] Toward the end of her remarkable life, a group of young pastors who had been mentored by her and who greatly admired her Christian stature and leadership asked her if there was anything she would do differently if she were to do it all over again. Without a moment of hesitation, she replied, "I would trust God more."[9]

When you first hear about her reply, you might think she was saying that in the hard, challenging periods of life, she wouldn't be so anxious. But it turns out she was thinking that she would have looked more for what could only be accomplished if God himself intervened to make it happen. She, who had such an amazing life of creative, effective ministry for God, wished she had trusted God even more.

Would you like to trust God more? Would you like to trust him more when life is tough? Would you like to attempt more for God that you know you could not pull off on your own? If so, I'd like to invite you to consider praying to ask God to grow your willingness to trust him when life gets tough and to encourage your willingness to take risks to advance his Kingdom. You could use this prayer or, if you prefer, create one like it in your own words:

Dear God,

You know and I know how much of my life I live without thinking I need to trust you or your direction for my life.

It's easy to realize that I need to trust you more when life is tough and I'm in over my head. But I'd like to learn how to risk more for you when my life is too comfortable.

I'd like to learn to trust you more when I'm at a fork in the road and more than one possible alternative for the road ahead looks attractive.

I'd like to learn to trust you more when the road I'm on ends and none of the alternatives ahead look good.

I'd like to learn to trust you more when it's time to leave the comfortable road I'm on and follow you in a different direction.

I'd like to learn to trust you more when I make choices (or have made choices) that aren't the best choices.

Thanks for your words to Peter: "Take courage. It is I. Do not be afraid." There are times when I need to hear those words, too.

Thank you for your presence in my life. I want to follow you and to trust you deeply with my life.

CHAPTER 4

Listening to God

We grow spiritually when we listen to God and to what he is trying to say to us. But often we are not very good at listening. Sometimes we think that the problem in communicating with God is how to get his attention when we have something to say to him or to ask him. Many people can identify with the person interviewed in the SG Project who said,

> *Prayer is hard for me; I've often felt like I was talking to a wall.*

Actually, God is already trying to communicate with us and we just don't realize it. It turns out that the real challenge is not how we can get God's attention but how he can get *our* attention. Another interviewee raised this same key question:

Listening to God. The word from my sabbatical was "Listen." And I'm still trying to work on that. How do you listen to God?

There are times when God just interrupts our lives, intruding to talk with us. On these occasions it's hard to miss the fact that he is talking to us (though we don't always understand what he is trying to say). But there are other times when God is much quieter, speaking with more of a whisper or a thought or a nudge. These whispers are easy to miss. And there are other occasions when God chooses to talk to us through other people. So how can we hear what he is trying to say to us?

God is God, but he is also your friend. He loves you and is delighted to be in relationship with you. He loves to be in conversation with you just like two friends might talk to each other. Figure 4-1 shows two friends talking over coffee. They are clearly enjoying the conversation. Their purpose is not to use the other person to get something they need. Rather, it's to share life and to enjoy the friendship. Suppose that you are one of those friends. You don't need to use any special vocabulary for your conversation (though you may have some words or phrases that are especially meaningful for the two of you). You don't need to say it just right. No conversational tricks are needed to get your friend's attention. You know each other; you've talked before. You don't have to worry about measuring up; you know you are accepted for who you are. You can share life, all of life, freely and openly. Sometimes you need to do more of the talking and your friend does a lot of listening. And sometimes your friend needs to talk and you do a lot of listening. But the key to a wonderful relationship is that each person knows how to listen. There are times when you have a hard time coming up with words to share what you are experiencing. It doesn't matter—your friend understands you and may even help you come up with words.

© Cathy Yeulet/123rf.com. Used by permission.

Figure 4-1. Conversation between Two Friends

Our conversations with God can also be like that, but unfortunately we often focus much more on talking to God than on listening to him. A number of years ago I had the opportunity to lead a seminar on prayer at a conference for people working with children in our church. There were some wonderful people there, including a friend who happened to sit off to the side of the room. I decided to have a little fun to illustrate a key point about prayer as more than a one-way conversation with God.

I walked over to my friend (let's call her Sharon) and told her I needed a penny. She dug into her purse, pulled out a penny and gave it to me. I thanked her and moved back to the front of the room. Then I turned around and went back to Sharon and asked her if she had a nickel or a dime she could give me. Again, she dug into her purse and pulled out a dime and gave that to me, too. I thanked her and started to walk away.

Then I turned back and asked her if she could give me a dollar. She had a puzzled look on her face, but being a very generous person, she gave me a dollar bill. Again I thanked her and turned to walk away. By this time I had the attention of everyone in the room; they were trying to figure out what was going on. But I thought I'd try one more time. I turned back to Sharon and told her I needed a mirror. I wasn't sure what she would do, but sure enough, she dug back into her purse and pulled out a mirror and gave it to me. I thanked her for the mirror and walked back to the front of the room. Then I asked those in the seminar what they thought about my "conversation" with Sharon.

As you can imagine, it was a great discussion about how I just talked, just asked for stuff and didn't take any time at all to listen for what Sharon was thinking or how she might want to enter into the conversation. I wonder how often our conversations with God are like this.

God wants a relationship with us and he delights in communicating with us because of that relationship. It turns out he is very creative and has a wide variety of ways to get our attention and to communicate with us.

When God Intrudes to Talk to Us

One way God can communicate with us is by interrupting us in the middle of the routines of our life when we aren't looking for him at all. We are not expecting God to talk to us; he just intervenes, and what he has to say can be quite disruptive. These times are much like the scene shown in Figure 4-2, where the batter is concentrating on his normal job of getting ready to hit the baseball when the pitcher throws it to him. But in the illustration, his routine is disrupted by a fan who has somehow walked onto the field and is tapping the batter on the elbow, wanting to speak to him. This interruption is unusual and unexpected.

Original photo © Dennis Ku/Shutterstock.com. Used by permission.
Intruding fan added digitally.

Figure 4-2. Interruptions

There are numerous examples in the Bible where God intruded into someone's routine to communicate and bring significant change. Mary, who became the mother of Jesus, experienced such an interruption by God in the middle of the routine of her young life.[1] She was engaged but not yet married when God sent the angel Gabriel to her to tell her that she would give birth to a son and that he should be named Jesus. The angel also said that her son would be great and be called the Son of the Most High and that God would give him the throne of David and his kingdom would never end. Wow! *There's* an interruption to the routine of life! Mary couldn't have known what all that meant, but she sure knew that, whatever it meant, the message was from God.

Peter, Andrew, James and John were busy working as fishermen when Jesus came by and invited them to leave their jobs and follow him (to a completely different job).² On another occasion, a woman was going about her routine task of drawing water at a well outside the city when a stranger (Jesus) interrupted her and began a conversation that changed her life.³ Then there was the man who had been an invalid for thirty-eight years and, as usual, was lying by the pool of Bethesda along with many other disabled people who were hoping for healing. One day, in the middle of this routine, Jesus came by and began a conversation that resulted in complete healing for the man.⁴

As a final example, think about the two men who were walking home from Jerusalem a few days after Jesus had been crucified. They were crushed. Their hopes had been dashed and they were thoroughly downcast about what had happened to Jesus. There were reports that Jesus had come back to life, but they had not seen him themselves. While they were walking home, Jesus himself joined them (though they did not recognize him in his resurrected body) and began a conversation. In this conversation Jesus explained what was said in all the Scriptures concerning himself. But they still did not know that this really was Jesus talking with them. As they approached their village toward evening, they urged him to stay with them, and at dinner, when Jesus broke bread and gave thanks for it, they finally realized who he was. Though he then vanished from their sight, they remarked about the conversation on the road home, saying, "Were not our hearts burning within us while he talked to us on the road and opened the scriptures to us?"[5] What a remarkable story of God's intrusion in their lives! Jesus was communicating with them and they didn't realize who it was at first. Each of these interruptions in life was at God's initiative and completely unexpected by those whose lives were so completely disrupted by God's intervention.

I had a personal experience of God's interruption a few weeks after completing the two hundred interviews for the SG Project. When I started the interviews, I didn't have any intention of writing a book. I expected to write a report on the results, but not a book. During the interviews, a number of people asked me if I planned to write a book, but I always replied no. True, the interviews were stunning in wisdom and insight, and I was increasingly aware that they were brimming with important material that could be the basis for a book. But I did not see myself as equipped to pull together this material and write a book that would capture what I was learning.

Then one night I woke up at one thirty with a torrent of great ideas related to the interviews. Not wanting to waste the ideas, I got up and spent an hour writing them all down. With a sense of relief at a task accomplished, I headed back to bed. But I had no sooner relaxed back in bed than I had a whole new set of great ideas. I got up once again and spent another hour writing them down. By then I found myself laughing; I began to sense that these really good ideas might be from God, and I felt the need to point out to God that I really did need to get some sleep. Then I headed back to bed. But again, just as I settled back against the pillow, I had still more great ideas. So I got up a third time to write so that these new ideas wouldn't be lost either.

These intrusions in the middle of the night left me with a strong sense that the flood of ideas must have been from God; the ideas were just that good. So I got the message and set out to write a book about what I was learning from all these amazing interviews.

It's not hard to listen when God intrudes so obviously in our lives. It really gets our attention and motivates us for action. We may not really understand all he has in mind, but we know that God has spoken.

Listening to God's Whispers

One morning I walked out of my house, closed the front door and headed across the driveway to my car. I was in a hurry because time was short and I did not want to be late for work, but I stopped to put a few things into the trunk of my car. For just a few moments, I paused and it was very quiet. I realized that I could hear a dog barking far in the distance. As I listened more carefully, I also heard not just one bird but a chorus of birds chirping. I had not heard these sounds at all when first walking out of the house. The sounds were there, but I had not heard them because they were so subtle and I was in such a hurry.

Sometimes God speaks to us in ways that are that subtle. Sometimes what he has to say to us is almost like a very soft whisper or a dad whispering in his child's ear in the middle of the cacophony of sounds on a carousel, as illustrated by Figure 4-3.

Photo by Jay Flaming.

Figure 4-3. Whispers

A thought comes to mind and we wonder if this is from God. We think we might be hearing God's voice, but we are not sure that it really is God talking to us. We wonder, "Is this God or not?" Sometimes we want to hear him loudly and clearly. Instead, all we hear is a deafening silence. But in the midst of that, a thought might cross our mind. It is subtle, but it won't go away. We wonder, "Is this maybe from God?" It is only afterward that we realize that the subtle whispers really were from God, but it wasn't at all clear at the time.

I remember a time when I was at a high school conference with students from our church. During an evening talk, I was standing at the back of the room with a few of the guys. It was a great talk, and as I looked out over the group, I had a sense that I wanted to be available for conversations with some of the students afterward. But no thought came to mind about what to do about it. As the meeting ended, I continued to look over the group. I was praying about what student I might talk to, but no one really seemed to stand out. After a few minutes of quiet, the guy standing right beside me asked, "Can you tell me how I could become a Christian?" He had been standing next to me during the whole talk, but I did not realize right away that God's whispers were about the guy standing right at my side.

On another occasion, on my way home from a small group meeting, I thought about visiting a friend who lived not too far off my normal route home. I hadn't set up a time to drop by and hesitated to bother him with an unexpected visit, but the thought wouldn't go away. After debating the issue over and over, I finally decided to at least stop by his house. It turned out he was home and we had a very meaningful visit, one that both he and I deeply valued. But I had almost missed God's whisper about visiting my friend.

A woman interviewed for the SG Project told me about getting subtle messages that she eventually realized were coming from God:

I realized that the Holy Spirit was really communicating with me. I would get these strong messages. Even as a kid, I had that but didn't know what it was. It starts with an openness to listening.

Sometimes God, even when subtle, can be very persistent in getting through to us. As one interviewee said:

I keep thinking that God is trying to get a particular thought across to me. He will keep pointing me to it over multiple times. The idea may come up in a range of ways— six or seven different things keep pointing to something.

Bill Hybels, founder of Willow Creek Community Church, near Chicago, has written a whole book about God's whispers. In his introduction to the book, titled *The Power of a Whisper*, he says:

When the sovereign God chooses to communicate with someone—whether eight, eighteen or eighty years old— that person's world is rocked. Without a hint of exaggeration, I can boldly declare that God's low-volume whispers have saved me from a life of sure boredom and self-destruction. They have redirected my path, rescued me from temptation and reenergized me during some of my deepest moments of despair. They inspire me to live my life at what boaters call "wide-open throttle"—full on![6]

He goes on to give example after example of amazing impacts from times when he has responded to God's whispering in his life, as well as reflections about God's whispering in our lives. It's an excellent book and fascinating to read.

Listening to God through Other People

We also hear God through other people. It might be through special friends who know us well, through someone in a small group or through a sermon. A good friend once told me that the voice of the Holy Spirit sounded suspiciously like the voice of his wife!

One person interviewed for the SG Project shared about a time when his life hit rock bottom, and God spoke to him through a co-worker:

> I was doing a lot of religious activity in my church. I started to see a few things. I knew what the right things were but just didn't choose to do them. I was still bent toward a sinful life. Then I hit rock bottom. One day I got a note from a secretary that said, "I'm praying for you." I knew it meant "You are messing up." That challenge encouraged me to make some right decisions that led me from a period of high spiritual decline to high spiritual growth.

Another interviewee talked about a conversation with a special friend who had been key in helping her see and take the next step in her life:

> When I came back to Seattle from the Peace Corps, I was thinking, "I don't know what I'm going to do." One day I walked around Green Lake with a good friend who knows me better than anybody, and I was thinking about what is next. She is great at asking questions. She strongly encouraged me to apply for a particular job. I did so and got the job.

And another described the impact of a pastor who brought healing and a challenge toward a new direction to her life:

> *I got a job as an admin for him. I was so healed while I*
> *was part of his ministry team. Then one day he said to me,*
> *"You need to be involved in full-time ministry."*

Shortly after finishing the last of the interviews for the SG Project, a friend asked how the project was going and I reported that I had just finished the interviews. She thought for a minute and then asked me two important questions: "What is happening to you personally as a result of all these interviews? What are the themes emerging from the research that you are becoming passionate about?" I replied that those were great questions but that I hadn't given them enough thought to give her much of an answer. Her questions really started me thinking about what was resonating personally as a result of the project and about the possibility of writing a book. Though I did not realize it at the time, I can now see that God used my friend to plant seeds that would grow into my willingness and passion to write this book.

God wants a relationship with you, and he delights in communicating with you in the midst of that relationship. Do you want to be the kind of person who listens to him? Do you wish that you could do better at listening to God when he wants to talk with you?

If so, you might ask God for help in listening to him and taking what you hear to heart. You could use the prayer below or, if you prefer, create one like it in your own words:

> *Dear God,*
>
> *I want to be the kind of person who listens to you.*
>
> *I really like the idea of just being able to talk with you as a friend.*

It's so great that I don't have to use religious words to talk to you—that I can just talk.

I'm glad you know me even better than I do, so you understand what I'm trying to say even better than I do myself.

But I also want to listen.

Would you help me grow in my ability to listen to you?

Would you help me to be more responsive to your whispers?

Would you help me to listen better for you in other people?

I'm pausing for a bit here to listen for you.

What do you have to say to me today?

CHAPTER 5

Listening for God

I live in a small town bordered by the main railroad tracks that run from Seattle to points north and east. A significant number of trains go by each day. Let's suppose I'm standing on Main Street near where it intersects the tracks and an eighty-car freight train is going by. The car barricades are down, the safety lights are flashing and the train makes a lot of noise as it thunders past. There is no doubt the train is there. I'm not anticipating the train; I'm experiencing it.

Now let's change the scene. Instead of standing at Main Street watching a train go by, suppose I'm three hundred feet south of Main Street at the train station (see Figure 5-1). I'm waiting for a train to arrive so I can climb aboard to travel to Canada. I've come to the train station because I know this is a very good place to catch the train. There is no train in sight yet, but I'm anticipating its arrival. I'm listening for the noise from the train but not hearing it yet. I'm looking for the train to appear around the corner in the distance, but I'm not seeing it yet. I'm not experiencing a train; I'm anticipating it.

Illustration by Abigail Platter.

Figure 5-1. Anticipating the Train

What does this illustration have to do with listening to God? There are times when God does interrupt to speak to us. He does whisper to us, sometimes persistently. And he does speak to us through other people. In these circumstances, we are not just anticipating God's talking to us; we are experiencing it. We are listening to God. It's happening. It's like the description above where I'm standing on Main Street watching the train actually going by.

But there are other times when we are listening *for* God. We are not yet hearing God speaking to us, but in anticipation, we can listen for God even before we hear him talking to us. It's like standing at the train station anticipating the arrival of the train.

Listening for God starts with our attitude. What is our attitude toward the coming year, month, week or day? Do we expect God to be at work in our lives and our world even before we see it happen? Do we expect him to be at work and to speak to us about what he is up to and to invite us to be part of that work?

One day when driving to work, I realized that I wasn't expecting God to do a single thing in or around my life that day. The events planned for the day were swirling through my mind, along with what I hoped to accomplish. I had a mental picture of how the day would play out, but there was no place in that picture for God; I had just left him out. My dismay at this realization grew stronger as I recognized that this was not unusual; on most days I didn't really expect to see God at work in my workplace.

To change how I viewed my day, I decided to put a note in a conspicuous spot on the dashboard of my car to remind me as I drove to work to listen for God, to expect him to be at work in my workplace. I intended this to help me work at proactive listening during the day, asking God what he was working on around me and what he wanted to say to me about the day. I did not want to just tell him about my day and ask for his intervention where I thought I might need his help for my agenda. I wanted to come to the day intentionally listening for God, pen in hand, sitting on the edge of the seat, ready to take notes. Instead of coming to God with a list in hand of what I intended to say to him, I wanted to be listening for him and expecting him to communicate with me.

One of the people interviewed for the SG Project commented

about this kind of proactive listening when sharing about a
period of high spiritual growth:

> *I was in a period of high* spiritual *growth again. I'm lis-
> tening to God; I'm constantly thinking, "What does the
> Lord have for me today?" And my growth is not just from
> understanding, but more personal.*

In our action-packed culture, it's hard to take time to listen to
the people around us, to really listen. How can we really hear what
is important to them? How can we really listen to what is on their
minds? How can we really listen to their hearts? Especially in our
culture, it is very important to learn how to really listen to our
children, to our spouses, to those around us and to God. It doesn't
happen by accident; it requires proactive listening.

In proactively listening for God, we take time to do things
that make us more likely to hear him. It's like the illustration at
the beginning of this chapter where, if I want to catch a train, I go
to the train station (because that's a good place to catch a train).

Jesus took time at key points in his life to go to a quiet place,
away from the activity and bustle of the town, to listen for God.
For example, in the middle of many miraculous healings at
Capernaum, he went at daybreak to a solitary place to listen for
God. Just before his arrest and crucifixion, he went out to a place
on the Mount of Olives (as usual) to pray about the events that
he knew would lead to his death. We, too, can get away to some
favorite quiet place to listen for God to speak to us alone. And
people sometimes go on prayer retreats with other people to get
away and consciously take time to listen for God.

Another great way to proactively listen for God is to read
Scripture. There are many valuable ways to read Scripture, but
some are particularly effective in helping us listen for God to

speak to us. In reading scripture to listen for God's message to us personally, the focus is not so much on studying a Scripture passage as on looking for the author (God) to speak to us out of the passage. We want to listen for the freshness of what God is trying to say to us today. This is very different from reading an encyclopedia to get information. In reading the Bible, we can expect that God will communicate with us personally through the words of the passage.

A number of years ago, I taught a short course related to electronics. The course focused on some technology so new that it was not in any textbooks, so I had written a short booklet on this material to go with my lectures. One evening in the middle of class discussion, I discovered an error in the book- let and explained to the class what the wording should have been. I remember with some amusement how some students just couldn't see how my explanation could be true, given that it didn't match what they could read in the printed booklet. Finally, I had the students turn to the title page that showed my name as the author. Then they realized that they were listening to the actual author explaining the concept, not just someone else try- ing to explain or correct what the author was saying. Reading the ⁹. Bible is like that, but in a much more powerful way. God himself, the inspiration behind the words in Scripture, can speak to us as we read the words to call our attention to what he knows we need to hear. We can expect that he will speak to us personally through the words we are reading. *But we need to recognized we are seeing through*

One way to help hear God's personal word to us as we read *God* the Bible is to use the following three questions suggested by Bruce Larson. These questions are helpful both for individual reading and for use in a group:

- What did I see in this passage that I'd never seen before about who God is?
- What did I see in this passage that I'd never seen before about who I am?
- What did I see in this passage that I'd never seen before about what God might be inviting me to do?

Another way of listening for God's personal words to us is known by the fancy name of *Lectio Divina*. This can be used either in a small group or individually. A short passage of Scripture is read out loud multiple times (usually three or four times) and a time of quiet personal reflection follows each reading. During a first reading, simply notice what word or phrase stands out to you. During a second reading, pay attention to any emotions or images that come up related to the word or phrase that stood out. During the third reading, consider if you sense any invitation in what you have been reflecting on. Finally, take a few moments just to rest in and experience God's love.[1]

You can also use a Scripture passage (such as a Psalm) as words of prayer for yourself. This provides a wonderful way to have a dialogue with God and to listen for words he would like to communicate to you.

Another good way to listen for God is a thirty-day listening experiment where you start each day by saying to God: "God, I'd like to listen for you today. What do you want me to hear?"

Journaling is another way that people find helpful in listening for God to speak. In writing out our thoughts and feelings, we sometimes discover the voice of God. One of those interviewed for the SG Project shared the value of journaling in helping her to listen for God's words to her:

This was the most critical, critical period in my adult life. I had a baby with colic. I felt trapped; I'm home with a child, but I've got a wide-ranging, curious mind. I was very vulnerable, and in the midst of that, my husband was not going to pursue the career we had been planning on. I'm thinking, "Where are you, God? What do you want me to do?" That's where really learning to listen began to happen. This is when I started dialogue journaling, writing down what I was hearing. So when I first started journaling, I did a lot of it with tears while my child was napping. I was writing about what I'd really like to do. God was clearing an emotional and spiritual path.

Another interviewee also shared her experience with journaling:

I worked at a church where the pastor was very affirming. I really started ramping up prayer. I worked more at listening and writing down what I was hearing.

How have you most often heard God's words to you? It might be valuable to think about how you have already heard from God and pay attention to those ways of listening.

Listening for God at Work in Other People

Another important aspect of listening for God is listening for him at work in the people around us. In this case we are listening not only to the words people are sharing but also for what God might be doing in them that prompts those words. The book of I Samuel in the Bible includes an instructive story about how God can use other people to help us hear his voice.[2] The story is about Samuel, a young boy who lived with and worked for Eli, the high priest, in the Temple at Shiloh. One night God called out to Samuel, calling him by name. Samuel heard God's voice but did not know it was God calling, so he ran to Eli and said, "Here I am; you called me." Eli knew he hadn't called Samuel and, at first, didn't know Samuel had heard God's voice. So he told Samuel to go back to bed. After this happened two more times, Eli realized that it was God who was calling and gave Samuel some great advice: he told Samuel to go back and lie down and if he heard someone calling again, he should say, "Speak Lord, for your servant is listening." Sure enough, God did call Samuel's name again. This time Samuel replied as Eli had suggested and had the opportunity to hear what God wanted to tell him. In listening to Samuel, Eli had noted that God was at work and helped Samuel listen to what God had to say.

One of those interviewed for the SG Project shared her experience of someone who noticed God at work in her life:

> I had my own kids and had this urge to go to church again. I was just floating and not involved in church. I had this powerful drive to go to church. So I did. While there, I told the pastor I wanted to be baptized. I got really sick for a week or so during this time, and the pastor would visit me leading up to baptism. I know I have to get baptized and do it now. I really knew nothing about denominations, but the pastor understood that I was having this encounter with God.

Asking questions can help us listen for where God is at work in other people. The effectiveness of these questions is not in our technique; it's in our listening heart and our openness to the Holy

Spirit's prompts as we are in conversation with other people. One Sunday after a worship service in a large church, I struck up a conversation with a couple I did not know who had been sitting in the row behind us. It was a delightful conversation, and I decided to ask them where they were experiencing the cutting edge of ministry for the Kingdom of God. I wouldn't ask this question of just any person I had just met, but I had the sense that the question might fit them. It turned out they had been thinking about that very question, and it led to a wonderful conversation where I could easily see how God was at work in their lives.

A few years ago my wife completed a two-year program that provided good training in how to listen for God at work in other people and how to help them learn to listen to God in their own lives. The description of this program includes the following important statement about how we can help each other listen for God in our lives:

> *We believe that meeting with another Christian brother or sister on a regular basis to attend to/pay attention to the present activity and prayer going on within your heart and soul is a spiritual discipline that grows the roots of our faith.*[3]

We really can help each other grow spiritually by listening for God in each other.

Listening for God outside My Agenda

We can expect God to be at work, but we also need to realize that there will be many times when it will be hard to recognize what God is up to, because his plans won't always make sense to us. God's plans may clash with our expectations or plans. This was the problem of the religious leaders of Jesus's day; they didn't recognize him as the Messiah they were looking for.

This was also Peter's problem when God wanted to send him to visit the Roman centurion Cornelius.[4] Peter's upbringing would have taught him not to visit a non-Jewish home or have dinner with a non-Jewish person. God had to give Peter the same jarring dream three times to get him ready to think outside his previous experience and agree to visit Cornelius.

We can get so locked into our agenda and become so sure that it is the same as God's that it can become very hard for us to hear God's agenda. A good example of this dilemma would be recent political campaigns where there were Christians on both sides of important issues. I had strong Christian friends on both sides, all of whom were passionate about their points of view, their agendas. These Christians on opposite sides were so sure that they were on God's side that it would have been hard for many of these folks to have heard God if his agenda had somehow been different from theirs. I'm sure God must have longed to get these Christians together in a room and say, "OK, I've heard your fervent, passionate prayers on both sides of these issues. I know your agendas. But here's mine. Here is what I'm up to and what I long to see happen. Will you follow me? Will you listen to me for my agenda?"

But aren't those questions that God asks all of us? How can God get our attention when we are locked into our own agendas and not listening for his? Of course, I already know what God's thinking will be. I'm already pushing for it. I am on God's side— on his agenda. It's folks on the other side who need to hear God talk about his agenda. Oops …

Sometimes God must take drastic action to get our attention.

This was certainly true for Saul of Tarsus when Jesus appeared to him on the road to Damascus.[5] Saul was thoroughly committed to imprisoning all the followers of Jesus he could get his hands on. He believed he was serving God by these actions. One day when Saul was on his way to capture some Christians in Damascus, he encountered a blindingly bright light and heard a voice say, "Saul, Saul, why do you persecute me?" Saul certainly did not expect to hear God asking him this question! Well, why *was* he persecuting God? It was because Saul had confused his agenda with God's. He thought he was following God's agenda, but in fact he was reading off the wrong page.

Like Saul, even when we really want to follow God's agenda, we sometimes make it very difficult for God to get through to us. At times God can't get our attention because we are stuck in a rut. We are "accustomed to doing it this way." At other times God can't get our attention because we have invested lots of time in a process or project and don't want to give it up or throw it away. And then there are the times when God can't get our attention because what he has in mind conflicts with what we believe is right or "the right way to do this." We can become so sure that what we are doing in God's name is the right thing that it is almost impossible for God to get through to us to tell us that he has something different in mind.

The solution is not that we should be weak or tentative or that we should not have an agenda. On the contrary, we should throw all our vision, energy and commitment into what we believe to be God's agenda for us. But in the process of carrying out that agenda, we always need to be receptive to the Holy Spirit for correction when we are off target or for adjustment to take advantage of the unexpected opportunity of the moment.

There are some pieces of God's agenda that he does not reveal in advance but only along the way. No matter how thoroughly we prepare or how intently we look to God in advance, there will be times when we need to change our plans to match the unexpected. As we are in the process of life, can we be available to God when he has something different in mind or when the unexpected occurs?

What can help us be interruptible for God's use and for his agenda? Although there is no magic formula, I think a number of suggestions are helpful. Probably most important is to remember that in any situation, God's agenda might be different from ours. It is also helpful to remember that in being interruptible for God's use, we will be *reacting* to some unexpected initiative or event; we can't plan for it in advance.

These interruptions from God catch us by surprise and catch us unprepared. At those moments, asking God for guidance and listening to his voice is especially important. I call it "praying in the process." When caught by surprise, we usually won't have any idea what to do or say, but we know that something is needed. While quickly sorting through the situation, we can ask God for special wisdom and insight. We can ask God to help us do what he has on his agenda even though we aren't sure what his agenda is in this particular situation. And as we pray, we can trust that the Holy Spirit will give us the words to say or guidance as to what to do. Last but not least, the people God has placed with us in ministry are often instrumental in helping us to be interruptible for his agenda. When we don't have an answer, they might. When we don't know what to do, they might. When we aren't hearing what God is saying, they might. We need to be listening to those God puts around us to bring us his wisdom.

Taking God's Words to Heart

In a number of Gospel accounts, Jesus concluded his teaching with the words "He who has ears to hear, let him hear." He meant much more than just physically hearing the words. He meant really getting it, taking his words to heart. His disciples often had a terrible time with this. They often heard his words and were confused. Sometimes they were sure they didn't understand and asked Jesus to explain what he was trying to communicate. And he then helped them comprehend what he had said.

In the book of Mark, we read about Jesus talking to his disciples and the gathered crowd. He tells them a parable about a farmer who went out to sow seeds in a field. The farmer planned for the seeds to take root and grow into plants that would create a wonderful harvest. But this did not happen for all the seeds. Some fell on hard ground and didn't grow much. Other seeds fell among thorn bushes that choked the new plants before they could mature. However, some seeds landed in good soil, soil that was ready to receive them and prepared to help the seeds sprout, take root, flourish and eventually produce a bountiful harvest.[6]

This parable has a lot to say about taking God's words to heart. Sometimes we just don't want to listen to God. Sometimes our hearts can be too hard for us to really hear, to get what God is saying to us. The words just bounce off. This was certainly true of many of the Pharisees at the time of Jesus. They were not ready to hear what Jesus was saying; they had hard hearts. At other times, we hear what God is saying, but we hear it only superficially and the words just don't take root. At still other times, we hear what God is saying and start to respond, but all the competing activities of life press in and we are too busy to give the words room to grow. But during the times when we really take God's word to heart, it can take root, grow and cause a significant impact both in our own life and in the lives of people around us.

What if God has something he would like to tell you or share with you? He almost certainly does! I invite you to pray to ask God for help in listening for him, listening to him and taking what you hear to heart. You could use the prayer that follows or, if you prefer, create one like it in your own words:

Dear God,

I want to be the kind of person who listens for you—who not just listens to you when you talk but listens for you even before I hear you speak to me.

Would you help me grow in my ability to listen to you and to listen for you?

I want to be someone who really hears and gets what you have to say to me.

I want your words to me to take root, to flourish, to grow and to multiply.

Would you help me to listen better for you in other people?

Would you help me to listen better for you outside my agenda?

I'm pausing for a bit here to listen for you.

What do you have to say to me today?

CHAPTER 6

Obeying God

Obeying God goes far deeper than just keeping some rules for good living. It has to do with our responses to God's prompts to do something as a result of listening for him and listening to him. How we respond can often have a significant impact on our spiritual growth. In fact, in the SG Project, "obeying God" was one of five factors that got top ratings for causing spiritual growth (see Figure B-1 in Appendix B).

But we often face major challenges in obeying God. Sometimes we simply prefer our way over God's way. Sometimes we can be immobilized by the risks we see in doing what we think God is asking us to do. Sometimes we don't have a clue about how what God is asking us to do fits into the larger picture of what God is doing. At other times, what God asks us to do doesn't make sense to us because God doesn't think like we do. Obeying God has to do with saying yes to God's prompts in spite of these challenges.

How Far Can You See?

Obeying God is often difficult because we can't see far enough ahead; we don't have a full picture of the future. This creates a challenge in obeying God; we need to decide to obey him in the next step even though we know we can't see the whole journey. One of the amazing accounts of obeying God without knowing what lay ahead is the story of Abram (later called Abraham).[1] Abram was seventy-five years old and lived in the city of Haran with his immediate and extended family. He had accumulated many possessions. It's safe to assume that Abram was very comfortable in Haran. But one day God told him, "Go from your country, your people and your father's household and go to the land I will show you." God didn't even tell Abram where he would be going! God just told him to leave the familiar Haran environment.

Abram had no idea what lay ahead. He did not know where he was going or even the next steps, only that God had promised to show him where he would be going and to greatly bless him. It's fun to picture the conversations Abram must have had with his wife and family about moving! Remarkably, in spite of the enormous uncertainty about the path ahead, Abram chose to obey God. He packed up his family and possessions and left Haran. The following chapters of Genesis tell an amazing story of how God did guide Abram and prepare him for the steps ahead. Abram lived to a very old age, and God did indeed bless him in every way.

I like seeing what lies ahead; I like the big picture. And I like context. When going to a new city, I like to go to the highest spot and look around, taking in the view. It might be the highest hill, or maybe a tall building or possibly a church tower. From there you can see how all the pieces of the city fit together.

But when following God, there is no way to see the whole context of a choice, to see the whole journey that lies ahead. All we can see is the next step we believe God is calling us to take.

Figure 6-1 shows a wonderfully adventurous scene. The skipper has steered the sailboat into just the right angle with the wind to get the maximum speed as it cuts through the water. But what particularly intrigues me about this photo is the land barely visible in the distance. It brings to mind a similar photo I saw many years ago, with these words printed across it in large letters: "Go as far as you can see. When you get there you will be able to see further."[2]

© *NatureDiver/Shutterstock.com. Used by permission.*

Figure 6-1. Go as Far as You Can See

This is the key to obeying God for the next step. We can't see the whole journey—we are not able to see what is in the distance. But we can choose to trust that God does see far ahead of us, and we can choose to obey him in taking the next step. After we take that next step, we will then be able to see what we couldn't see before.

The process whereby God used Moses to get the children of Israel out of Egypt is another fascinating example of obeying God one step at a time.[3] Before Moses became leader of the Israelites, he worked for his father-in-law, taking care of a flock of sheep. One day while Moses was at work, God sent an angel in the form of flames of fire from within a nearby bush. But the flames weren't destroying the bush. Being very curious, Moses decided to move closer to this strange sight. When he approached it, God called to him from within the bush, saying, "Moses! Moses!" Moses must have been very surprised, but he replied, "Here I am." God proceeded to tell Moses he was sending him to the Pharaoh of Egypt to ask that the enslaved Israelites be allowed to leave Egypt. God told Moses that it wasn't going to be an easy task but that in the end, Pharaoh would agree to let the Israelites go. Moses was not comfortable with any part of what God had in mind, but after quite an extensive discussion with God, Moses chose to do what God was asking him to do.

He went with his brother Aaron to tell Pharaoh that the God of Israel was telling him to let the Israelites go. Pharaoh refused and mocked the God of Israel. Indeed he took steps to make the lives of the Israelites even more miserable. So at God's direction, Moses and Aaron went again to Pharaoh and performed the first sign that God had told them to do: Aaron threw down his staff and it became a snake. But Pharaoh still did not listen. A series of meetings with Pharaoh followed. Each time, God sent Moses and Aaron to Pharaoh with instructions on what to say, including threatening a plague on Egypt if Pharaoh did not let the Israelites go. Each time, Pharaoh refused and God sent an additional plague in response. The plagues included turning the Nile into blood, sending frogs to cover the land, killing all the Egyptian livestock, sending boils to cover people and animals and sending the most violent hailstorm Egypt had ever seen. Finally, in the last plague, all the first-born sons in Egypt died, and Pharaoh and the Egyptians felt compelled to allow the Israelites to leave.

In each of the conversations with Pharaoh, Moses and Aaron had known only the next step; they had not known the whole process. But they obeyed God each time. And eventually, as God had said, the Israelites were set free from Egypt.

God Doesn't Think Like We Do

Our problem is more than just not being able to see far enough ahead. We often find it difficult to obey God because we don't think like he does. Since God is God, we can expect that his thoughts, perspective, actions and plans are much bigger than we can humanly comprehend. In the book of Isaiah, we find these important words that the prophet proclaimed in speaking for God:

> *"For my thoughts are not your thoughts, neither are your ways my ways," declares the Lord. "As the heavens are higher than the earth, so are my ways higher than your ways and my thoughts than your thoughts."*[4]

What an understatement! How true this is!

The problem is not just that God thinks farther ahead or that his thoughts are bigger than ours; his thoughts and ways are also altogether different and unexpected. Though not everything that sounds crazy is of God, there are times when God asks us to do things that might seem very strange.

From the Bible we know that the Israelites did not recognize God's agenda in the recommendation by Joshua and Caleb to walk into their "promised land" and instead listened to the majority report brought by the ten others who said the obstacles were too great.[5] The Syrian commander Naaman was incredulous when he heard that to be cured of his long-lasting leprosy, all he had to do was wash himself seven times in the dirty Jordan river.[6] Gideon was puzzled again and again as God kept reducing the size of his task force from an initial thirty-two thousand men to only three hundred when they headed out to fight the huge Midianite army.[7]

Looking at the life of Jesus gives us a bit of a window into the breathtaking unexpectedness of what we can experience from being around God. Jesus often interacted with people in unexpected ways. On one occasion, some folks were bringing little children to Jesus just to have him touch them. Not realizing how important children were to Jesus, the disciples rebuked those bringing the children. When Jesus saw this, he was indignant, and his response to the disciples was not at all what they had expected:

> *Let the little children come to me, and do not hinder them,*
> *for the kingdom of God belongs to such as these. Truly I tell*
> *you, anyone who will not receive the kingdom of God like*
> *a little child will never enter it.*[8]

On another occasion, a Pharisee named Nicodemus came to Jesus at night (so they could speak in private) and said that he knew Jesus was a teacher who had come from God. Jesus

answered him by saying that no one can see the Kingdom of
God unless he is born all over again. Nicodemus, though a religious teacher, couldn't grasp the answer; it was just too unexpected. Nicodemus couldn't believe what he was hearing:

> *"How can someone be born when they are old?" Nicodemus*
> *asked. "Surely they cannot enter a second time into their*
> *mother's womb to be born!"*[9]

So Jesus had to explain how a human being can enter the Kingdom of God.

Then there was the day when Jesus walked by a beggar sitting
by the side of the road. The man was blind; in fact, he had been
blind since birth. Jesus stopped as he came near the man and spit
on the ground to make some mud from the saliva. Then Jesus put
some of this mud on the blind man's eyes. Can you imagine what
the blind man might have been thinking? He certainly couldn't
have expected these unusual actions and must have wondered
what Jesus was trying to do. After putting the mud on the man's
eyes, Jesus told him to go wash it off in the pool of Siloam (the
name of the pool happened to mean "sent"). Remarkably, the
blind man did what Jesus told him to do—he went to the pool
and washed his eyes. To his amazement, he could then see! His
healing was so unexpected that some people who knew him
couldn't believe they were looking at the same man.[10]

In all these instances, being willing to do it God's way, even
though it seemed strange, allowed God to work through people
to accomplish what would have been impossible on any agenda
except God's. Clearly, God often does things in ways we would
never expect. When we are available for his agenda, we can be
sure that God will call us to do some things that don't seem
to make sense (at least not at the time). Certainly, asking what

makes sense in a given situation is an excellent guide for deci-
sion-making, but we also must be prepared to obey at those times
when God's agenda doesn't seem to make sense to us.

During her interview for the SG Project, Lori shared a
remarkable story about a difficult choice she had to make when
deciding to obey God's prompting:

> One day when in my late thirties, I was taking a walk
> and I was just communing with God. I felt him speak to
> my heart and say, "Write a tribute letter to your father." I
> definitely wasn't ready to do that. You see, when I was a
> kid, my dad had left us for another woman, and she left
> her family for him. The other woman had two children;
> my father had four children. Our lives were devastated.
> Everything that I had going on in my life that brought me
> joy no longer brought joy. My dad had devastated my life,
> and it took me a long time to recover from that.
>
> My dad didn't hear much from me over the years because I
> didn't really have a relationship with him other than send-
> ing him a Father's Day card, a birthday card or a Christmas
> card. I did long to have a relationship with him, but I didn't
> know how. I felt that he would judge me or I would judge
> him. We really didn't know each other very well any longer.
>
> So when God asked me to write that tribute letter, I had
> quite a bit of anxiety in my heart. I thought to myself, "He's
> really hurt me." I didn't really know what to say. But I
> went home and I put some pieces of paper together and
> grabbed a pencil. I said, "Lord, help me write this." As I
> obeyed God to write the letter, it brought back all the won-
> derful things my dad had done with me. I have to say that

the woman I've become today is a result of the things that my dad had taught me. So I said that in the letter. It was close to Father's Day, so I sent him this letter for Father's Day. But I heard nothing back from my dad.

It turned out that shortly after Father's Day there was going to be a big retirement party for my dad. I called my stepmother secretly and said, "Don't tell my dad, but I'm going to come to his retirement party." He lived in the Midwest and I lived out here in Seattle. But I did go to his retirement party. When I arrived, he was so glad to see me; he was just beaming and we embraced each other. He showed me an envelope, and I realized that he had brought my letter with him. He said, "It took me three hours to read this letter; I couldn't stop crying." As it turned out, my Dad had become a Christian. He embraced me again and asked, "Will you forgive me?"

A month later I got a phone call; it was my uncle Jim. He said, "I have to give you the news that your dad died today from a heart attack." It had been only one month since I had seen him; it was a complete surprise. The Lord knew what he was doing when he asked me to write that letter because otherwise I could be standing here today not having reconciled with my dad and having both of our spirits still wounded.

What God had invited Lori to do was not easy for her, but she wrote the letter out of obedience. And God used that obedience in a remarkable way. God's timing and Lori's willingness to obey God's prompt were both amazing.

Saying Yes to God

Obeying God has to do with saying yes or no to God's prompts. Bruce Larson explained it this way:

> *In our relationship to God we realize that the good news is not our response to a doctrine or a theology, but a response to a person. The gospel is embodied in a person affirming us: Jesus Christ saying, "I love you unconditionally. Will you give me your life?" ... We can only say "yes" or "no." To say yes is to return affirmation with affirmation. We affirm God by yielding to him, even as He had affirmed us by giving us himself in the person of Jesus Christ.*[11]

OK, after reading this chapter you may be thinking, "Well, I see the importance of following God's prompts, and I like the blessings from God that come from obeying them. But to be honest, I certainly haven't always said yes to God. What about me?" It is for you, dear reader, that I write the last words in this chapter. They are very important.

None of us is able to follow God's prompts all the time. Sometimes we don't obey because we don't hear God's prompting. But there also are times when we choose not to follow God. What happens then? At this point the experience of Peter on the night before Jesus was crucified can be very important to us—painful, but helpful. Peter was one of the three disciples closest to Jesus, and when the soldiers came to arrest Jesus, Peter was ready to fight for Jesus. Nonetheless, Jesus was arrested. Later that evening, as Jesus was being questioned by the religious authorities, Peter denied three times that he even knew Jesus. After the third time, Jesus turned and looked him in the eye.

Peter was devastated; he went outside and wept bitterly. Later that day Jesus was crucified by Roman soldiers and his body was placed in a tomb. All the disciples were devastated, but it must have been especially awful for Peter.[12]

Fortunately, there's more to the story. The death of Jesus was not the final word; God raised Jesus from the dead, and after his resurrection, Jesus appeared numerous times to the disciples and other followers. In one of these encounters, Jesus specifically reached out to Peter. In this interaction, Jesus asked Peter three times, "Simon, son of John, do you love me?" Each time Peter affirmed that he loved Jesus. It was painful for Peter to be asked this question three times, but in this way Jesus personally restored their relationship and confirmed Peter's leadership role in the early community of followers of Jesus.[13]

The wonderful news is that none of us are ever beyond God's forgiveness and grace if we choose to accept them. God's love and grace are that big! God is looking for us. We are not on God's blacklist; we are on his love list.

Do you wish to obey the prompts of God in your life? Do you long to know the love of God for you even when you fail to follow his prompts? If so, I invite you to pray the following prayer or create one like it in your own words:

Dear God,

Thank you for your wonderful affirmation that you love me unconditionally.

I do want to say yes to you, to give you my life, to yield my life to you. I want to follow your prompts in living out my life.

It's amazing that you know me even better than I know myself. And I know that you see further and better than I do—that you have the big picture.

Help me to risk following your prompts, to say yes to you and to trust you in taking those steps.

Lord, you know there are times when I fail to follow your prompts. I wish that weren't the case, but I know it is. I ask for your forgiveness for those times and ask you to help me believe I'm forgiven and to trust your grace.

Thank you for your amazing love!

CHAPTER 7

Getting Stretched

To grow spiritually, you have to get stretched beyond your comfort zone. It's that simple. You won't grow inside your comfort zone. At times we can get ourselves out of a comfortable rut, but when we live following God, we can be sure he will provide plenty of occasions to stretch us beyond where we are comfortable.

Many years ago when I was a stranger in a large city, I visited a church for Sunday worship. The worship service was OK, but what I remember most was the time after the service when groups of people were standing around talking to each other. I don't know that this was at all fair, but I imagined that these people were discussing rather superficial matters. When reflecting on this experience that afternoon, a parody of Psalm 23 ran through my mind. It went like this:

The Lord is my shepherd;
I shall not want.
I live only in green pastures.
I venture only near the still waters.
It rusteth my soul.

While this is certainly not the point of Psalm 23, the lines above do include some truth: if we experience only comfort in life, if we do not get stretched or challenged, our souls definitely will rust. One of those interviewed in the SG Project pointed out the importance of getting stretched with these words:

> *If we don't try new things or do new things, we will stay pretty much the way we are. If the Spirit gives direction, you want to go there. Our tendency has to be to say YES.*

Trying new things always involves risk, and that can make us uncomfortable. However, as the remarkable Swiss Christian physician Paul Tournier has pointed out, pursuing the adventure of life requires willingness to take these risks:

> *Life is a constant game of double or nothing. We are always tempted to save what we have by refusing to put it at risk again. But this means the end of adventure.*[1]

Stretching from Obeying God

Obeying God often involves choices that move us away from our routines, out of our comfort zones. The Gospel of Matthew tells about the day Jesus walked by a tax collection booth where Matthew was in the middle of an ordinary day at work.

His comfortable routine was completely interrupted when Jesus walked up and said, "Follow me." In response, Matthew got up, left his tax collecting job and followed Jesus. It completely changed Matthew's life.[2]

Remember how the Book of Acts describes Saul's first encounter with Jesus?[3] Saul was a strong opponent of those who had become followers of Jesus. He felt so strongly about stopping this dangerous movement that he persecuted and imprisoned any followers of Jesus he could find in his city of Jerusalem. Then one day on a trip to another town to capture more Christians, Saul encountered Jesus himself. At first, Saul could not make sense of this encounter because it was so different from the religious routine he knew. But eventually he did change direction to follow Jesus, and Jesus changed his life.

One of the interviewees in the SG Project reflected on her college experience, where she felt God's push to step up to new things:

At college, more than any other place, I could see God pushing me harder and harder. I was being pushed to step up to something that a year earlier I wouldn't have thought I could do.

Another interviewee, Ann, shared a wonderful story about how she, too, felt God's push to step up to something she wouldn't have thought she could do. She sees herself as an introvert, a person who processes by thinking rather than by talking and who needs time to sit and think all by herself. She said that one Sunday afternoon she had come home from a women's conference and was alone at home. It was just what she needed, after so much input, to have time to reflect on the conference she had just experienced. But the outcome of this reflection time surprised her; her most memorable thought from that afternoon seemed totally random, with no obvious relationship to the conference she had just attended. This is the thought that came to her: "You could teach fourth grade girls in Sunday School next year!"

She was just finishing her fourth year of working with toddlers and preschoolers at her church, but she had no experience at all with elementary children. None. Nevertheless, the idea of teaching fourth grade girls wasn't completely irrational. Her daughter was going into fourth grade, and she had thought it might be fun to be part of her daughter's Sunday School class. Ann also realized that there probably wouldn't be very many more years that her daughter would be thrilled to have her mom in her class. She became so excited about her idea on that quiet Sunday afternoon that she finally had to get paper and a pen to write down all her ideas about what she would do if she taught fourth grade girls.

But by the next morning she was thinking quite differently. She was sure she wouldn't be good at teaching fourth grade girls. She didn't do crafts, and she didn't do music. She remembered that she wasn't really attracted to elementary children, especially not groups of them. And it occurred to her that they probably wouldn't like her either. Over the next few weeks, she had two conflicting sets of thoughts: "You could teach fourth grade girls" and "You wouldn't be any good at it and they wouldn't like you."

Then one day while reading her Bible, she came to this sentence in Paul's second letter to the church in Thessalonica:

With this in mind, we constantly pray for you, that our God may make you worthy of his calling, and that by his power he may bring to fruition your every desire for goodness and your every deed prompted by faith.[4]

These words caught her attention. It seemed to her that God was telling her to pursue the good purpose he had planted in her heart and that he was promising to fulfill it through his power. She was able to let go of her worries about being inadequate to the task because God had promised her that he would make her class count for his Kingdom through his power, not her adequacy. So she phoned her Children's Ministries director and said she would love to teach fourth grade girls the next year if there were an opening. As it turned out, there was an opening and she taught that class for several years until she moved to another city. This is how she summarized her experience teaching fourth grade girls:

The four years I taught the fourth grade girls were the most amazing and wonderful experience I have ever had in ministry. How could something as simple and ordinary as teaching a kids' Sunday School class have had that kind of impact on me? I don't know; I only know it is one of the few times in my life that I have had such a strong sense of being called by God to do something.

I grew more in my relationship with God than almost any other time in my life as each week I would ask him what we were going to do next and he would give me ideas, and I believe that lives were touched by his power. Even now, whenever I see one of my "fourth grade girls" (who are now adults, many with families of their own), I realize again how much I still care about each of them.

Stretching from Risking for God

Bruce Larson often asked people, "What would you attempt for God if you knew you could not fail?" It wasn't intended as a rhetorical question to provoke sharing or discussion. It was a way to help us think outside our comfort zones, to consider that some of the wild, crazy ideas that occur to us might be from God. And God is looking for people to attempt some wild ideas. He doesn't need people who know they can pull them off; God will supply what it takes. But God does need people who are listening for his voice in the middle of wild, crazy ideas. To be sure, not all wild and crazy ideas are from God, but some will be. So what would you attempt for God if you knew you could not fail? You can have that conversation with God as you listen for his prompting. One of the interviewees in the SG Project shared this example of taking a risk to start out in a new direction:

> I'm starting nursing school. It's based on thinking, "If I could do anything, what would I do?"

Larson also talked about a challenge from God to be involved in the world around us:

> Finally God says, "Will you get out and be involved someplace in the world? Will you try to walk my love, my Word, my character to somebody? Will you lose your life? Yes or no?"[5]

Mission trips can be a very effective way of stretching our view of the world and what God is up to in it. And they can be a very effective way of stretching us beyond our comfort zones. As one of the interviewees said:

> Going on a mission trip to another country was profound

because it was outside my normal. But God was the same God. I saw God in more profound ways because of this mission trip.

Another person also commented on the huge growth that resulted from an extended mission trip:

I went on a study cruise with about fifty other people. That summer I almost exploded with painful growth. On this cruise, we were in eleven countries in seven weeks. You get a bunch of people away in a new environment—you're not only learning ideas, you're putting them into practice.

Of course, not all risks in life result in spiritual growth. Life is full of risks. Walking across a street is a risk. Riding in a car is a risk. Investing in a stock is a risk. As one interviewee noted:

Jumping out of an airplane without a parachute is taking a risk, but it may not result in spiritual growth.

But as we risk for God outside our comfort zones, we almost always experience spiritual growth. How much growth we experience depends a lot on how big the risk is. Small risks generally produce small growth. But if our risking for God is big enough to need his help to pull it off, it is the kind of risk that causes significant spiritual growth.

Are you attempting only things you know you can pull off on your own? Or are you attempting some things that could happen only if God shows up and enables it to happen?

Stretching from Significant Involvement

We are called to significant involvement to advance the Kingdom of God, not token involvement. Significant involvement can occur anywhere we find ourselves or choose to go. It can be in the world outside our country, somewhere in our country, in our city, in our neighborhood, at our place of work or within our church family. Wherever it is, we need to *choose* to work at being available for God's use. We need to have this desire as a high priority to guide our actions and vision for what God might do through us. To be deeply committed to God in ministry means throwing ourselves wholeheartedly into our place of ministry. As the letter to the Colossians puts it, "Whatever you do, work at it with all your heart, as working for the Lord."[6]

I am not arguing for Type A Christianity, where each Christian must be compulsively overworked in ministry. Rather, I'm suggesting that every Christian should have at least one place where his or her involvement is intense enough to make an impact for the Kingdom and to be a place of personal stretching and growing. There will be times in our lives when we need to take steps to become significantly involved, to find a place where we can be available for God to use us for his Kingdom. Token effort, even sustained token effort, does not result in growth or make much of an impact for the Kingdom. Furthermore, it's rarely much fun. But it does consume time and therefore sometimes gives us a misleading sense that we are significantly involved for God.

Often, places of ministry involvement ask very little of us. I can remember many times when someone has asked someone else to be involved using language like this: "It really won't take much time. All you need to do is ..." Such an approach is almost always a mistake. If the task really is that small, the involvement won't cause much stretching or growth. Worse, the vision for what God might do through the task is too small. People respond to the vision that is painted for them when asked to do something. So, if too small a vision is painted, there is often disappointment later at the small commitment people show for the task. But what they are doing is exactly what was asked, which was too little.

Other places of involvement do ask for a significant amount of time but the tasks lack the depth and vision necessary to make much of an impact. It is hard to be enthusiastically committed to a ministry that takes lots of time but doesn't seem to have much of a Kingdom vision or impact.

Even when we find a place of involvement where we can risk and get stretched and grow, we may not recognize it as such at first. Often it is only after we have been involved in a place of ministry for a while that it becomes really significant. We have to stay with it long enough to get past the dabble stage in order to grasp the opportunities and depth of ministry possible. And we need to stay with an involvement long enough to develop a vision for how to strengthen its impact for the Kingdom of God. The Kingdom is greatly blessed when we stay involved long enough to learn how to share what we are learning with others, helping them to get involved and helping them risk and grow.

I believe it is unhelpful and unwise to use the term *volunteers* for those who are not paid when involved in ministries for the Kingdom. In many secular organizations, the term *volunteer* refers to someone who is not part of the regular paid staff and implies less of a commitment than regular staff and often suggests less expertise. The term also suggests that the volunteer is only an assistant and therefore is given less responsibility.

These images produced by the term *volunteer* are not appropriate for the Church. Most people God uses for ministry are not paid and so in that sense are indeed volunteers. But as Christians, we are called to grow into expertise; we are called to develop vision, leadership and passion for our place of ministry and to grow into being more than just dabblers with limited commitment, expertise and vision. For this reason, one congregation that I know in Seattle has chosen the slogan "Every member a minister" to emphasize that ministry is not intended to be limited to paid staff but rather carried out by the whole congregation. It is a wonderfully radical concept. God intends each of us to grow into expertise in ministry and not be just observers or dabblers.

The significance of our involvement in a ministry depends on how much time we invest in it, how it ranks among our life priorities and the extent to which we are influencing other people to become involved or to grow in it. Typical levels of involvement vary from occasional to a focused regular commitment that is a center of passion, vision and leadership (see Figure 7-1). Although a person could be marginally involved in many ministries, it would be impossible to be very heavily involved in many at the same time (maybe only one).

The amount we are growing as Christians depends on the depth of our involvement, not on how busy we are. The more deeply involved we are, the more we grow. With token involvement, we grow very little if at all. For most people, significant growth does not occur until they are "quite involved." But when deeply committed to God, we usually grow even more than we believe possible. In addition, being deeply committed to God usually means that people around us grow as well. We have an impact on them as they see us growing and being used by God to make an impact for his Kingdom. There is nothing more deeply satisfying than when we realize we have been the right person in the right place at the right time doing the right thing to have an impact for the Kingdom of God.

Marginally Involved:
  • I help out in some way about once each year.
  • I am supportive of what this ministry is doing.

Somewhat Involved:
  • I believe in this ministry enough to commit a certain amount of regular time to it. I help out about once a month.
  • I am supportive of what this ministry is doing and enjoy talking to other people about it.

Quite Involved:
  • I am committed to spending regular time in this ministry at least twice a month.
  • This is one of several ministries in which I'm involved.
  • I am very supportive of what this ministry is doing and enjoy talking to other people about it.

Very Involved:
  • This is a ministry focus for me. I'm involved in this ministry about once a week.
  • I enjoy helping other people get involved in this ministry.

Very Heavily Involved:
  • This is a ministry focus for me. It is a center of passion, vision and leadership for me.
  • I'm involved in this ministry at least once a week.
  • I'm helping other people get involved in this ministry.
  • I enjoy helping other people grow in this ministry.

Figure 7-1. Levels of Ministry Involvement

What is your level of involvement in ministry to advance the Kingdom of God? Are you involved in a place of ministry where you are being stretched and are growing? Do you sense that God might be calling you to some new risk in a new ministry involvement? Or do you have a sense that God might be calling you to a new risk to try something for God in a ministry where you are already involved?

Maybe you would like to ask God to help you to deepen your level of involvement in serving him. If so, you could pray the following prayer or one like it in your own words:

O God,

I want to grow spiritually. But I realize that to do this, I will need to be stretched beyond my comfort zone.

Would you help me to be willing to be stretched by obeying you?

Would you help me to be willing to be stretched by risking for you to advance your Kingdom?

I'm amazed and distressed at how easy it is to dabble in your Kingdom business rather than to be fervently committed to it. But I want you to be the center of my life and I want to be passionately committed to some place of ministry to advance your Kingdom.

Would you lead me to a place of significant involvement for you?

What could I attempt for you that would be beyond my

ability to pull it off on my own, something where I would have to depend on you to make it possible?

And I pray that you will intervene in my life at those times when I need your help to restore my passion for you and for your Kingdom.

CHAPTER 8

Supportive Community

S ome people grow spiritually in isolation, without a supportive community, but more often people around us are an important influence for our spiritual growth. At the beginning of life, this can be our family of origin. Later it can be a youth group. Sometimes it can be a wonderful friend. Other times it can be a small group or a ministry team.

Supportive community can be a place where we are known *and* loved. It can be a place where we experience care, especially in the middle of a life crisis. It can be a source of affirmation. It can be a place where we are challenged to risk or to move ahead. Sometimes it can be a place where we have accountability.

In the SG Project, "supportive community" was one of five closely ranked factors with top ratings for impact in causing spiritual growth (see Figure B-1 in Appendix B). Furthermore, "supportive community" was reported significantly more often than any other cause of spiritual growth during high to medium spiritual growth periods (see Figure B-3 in Appendix B).

Supportive community was the spiritual growth approach that Jesus used. Reggie McNeal, a former pastor and author, has some key words about how Jesus shaped the spiritual growth of his disciples:

> *The organic community is the most critical aspect in shifting or shaping the corporate culture of your ministry. This was the primary approach used by Jesus. He lived with his disciples. This allowed him to debrief their lives and ministry assignments. In effect, he taught them how to learn from life and ministry. He sent the Holy Spirit to be their ongoing coach when he ascended back to the Father.*[1]

Real Christian Community Goes Deeper Than Chitchat

Christian community means much more than what many of us picture when we hear the word *fellowship*. For me, *fellowship* is an important Christian word that has become trite due to shallow implementation. It is a good word, I know, but it bothers me nonetheless. It suggests to me a scene where people are standing around drinking coffee or tea and chatting without much depth of interaction. Of course, many of us who are adults thoroughly enjoy talking to people in a relaxed setting. Sometimes the conversations are about things that really matter in people's lives and for the Kingdom—but often it seems to be only rather superficial chitchat.

Christian community means something much stronger; Christian community has to do with our awareness that we belong together, that we care for each other and are cared for, that we are known and we know those around us, that we share each other's joys and hurts and that we are working at affirming, supporting and encouraging each other's risking for the Kingdom of God. To maximize our effectiveness in advancing God's Kingdom, we need to have a sense of love and support, of affirmation and encouragement and belonging.

People long for this depth of supportive community. When they find it, it is a powerful propellant for spiritual growth. But it takes a lot of effort to make this level of supportive community happen, and many people have yet to find it. Instead, they experience only superficial relationships. Rather than getting to know the real person, they encounter a stick figure (see Figure 8-1).

Photo on the right © Viorel Sima/Shutterstock.
Used by permission.

Figure 8-1. Getting to Know the Real Person

As the interviewer for the SG Project, I had amazing opportunities to hear people talk about their lives from birth to present and to discuss the causes of spiritual growth over the course of time. I knew many of the people I interviewed, but it was stunning to see how many important things I had not known about them before these in-depth interviews.

How Much of a Person Do You Know?

People long for supportive community and would like to know real people, not just stick figures. But often only a small part of who we are gets shared with other folks at church. (See Figure 8-2 below.)

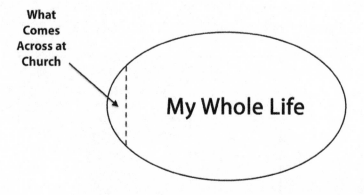

Figure 8-2. How Much of a Person Do You Know?

Why does so little of who we are get shared with other folks at church? I see at least four reasons. The first is that it takes some significant interaction to get beyond the superficial, beyond the stick figures. It often does not feel like there's enough time to develop a meaningful connection. And it does take some time; the real person may not be at all like our first impression.

After graduating from college, I spent a summer on the Lower East Side of Manhattan. I had gone to New York with three other people from Seattle to be part of a team of forty young people working with inner-city children. We spent the first two weeks being oriented to New York City. As usual in the summer, the weather in the city was uncomfortably hot and humid. After braving the heat for the first two days, one of my Seattle friends told me he was thinking of cutting off the legs of his jeans and wearing these cutoffs along with a T-shirt and sandals. He asked if I would do the same thing so he wouldn't be the only person on our team dressed so casually. I was hesitant at first but finally agreed because I knew it would be so much more comfortable.

We found a pair of scissors, cut off the legs of our jeans and showed up at the orientation the next day wearing cutoffs, T-shirts and sandals. The following orientation days were also hot and humid, and we continued to dress in the same light and casual manner. However, the other thirty-eight people on the team continued to dress more formally, so my friend and I stood out as unusual. Dressing much more casually kept us quite comfortable and also gave us unusual freedom in relating to other people on the team. We could easily strike up a conversation with people we did not yet know and then introduce them to others on the team. We became relational catalysts, breaking the ice to help people get to know each other. It was a delightful experience both for the team and for us.

However, the picture that others in the group were forming of me was quite incomplete and quite different from the more complicated picture I had of myself. I knew I was not as comfortable initiating conversations with new people as it seemed, and I knew I was certainly not as carefree as it appeared. Basically, I was playing a role that was only partially me. To be sure, it was a delightful role and very much appreciated by others on the team, but there was a difference between who I really was and who the other team members thought I was.

This disparity became clear a month after the summer ended when two women from the New York team came to visit Seattle. My friend and I had invited them to meet us at the main door leading into our church building. We were waiting at the door, and many other people were standing nearby talking. This was in the sixties, when people dressed up for church. Most of the men wore white shirts and ties; some had suit coats. When the two women came inside, their eyes opened wide with shock. When we asked what they were noticing, they replied with astonishment, "All the men have white shirts and ties!" We realized, to our amusement, that they thought that everyone in Seattle walked around in cutoffs, T-shirts and sandals! They clearly had formed a very incomplete picture of how people in Seattle dressed and who we really were.

A second reason we share only part of our life is that it is easy to think that in a church setting, our focus should be on only the religious dimensions of who we are. But there are many other dimensions to our lives. The following questions can be helpful in exploring them:

- What gave me great delight last year?
- What do I hope happens this year?
- What do I fear most?

- What do I enjoy about the work I do?
- What are my favorite hobbies or non-work activities?
- Where else in the world have I lived or visited?
- Who are my friends outside of church?
- What sports do I like?
- What is my favorite color?
- What are some of my favorite places in the city or town where I live now?

We could significantly broaden and deepen our supportive communities at church if we explored questions like these with each other.

A third reason we share so little is that church often seems to be about being "good." People may be afraid that if they share enough to let folks really know them, they might not fit in. One of the people I interviewed shared an important story that illustrates the tension that can occur between who we know we are and what we think other people might be expecting us to be:

> *Our family attended church each Sunday; in fact, we went to church three times a week. I began teaching Sunday School when I was thirteen or fourteen. But it was a hard time for me spiritually because my church friends were not my school friends. I felt like I was in two different worlds. So my spiritual interest lagged. My sister got involved in Young Life, and I got involved some but never went to camp. In college I really got into the social thing. I would be in church, but only to be seen there (and to make up for my sins).*
>
> *After college, I got a job and was on a high growth curve, though I was still mixed up trying to find out who I was.*

One summer my sister asked me to drive with her and a
friend out to Young Life's Frontier Ranch in Colorado. We
got to the ranch and I saw people I had known back at the
Young Life club in high school. I knew I was the prodigal
coming home. I thought, "Do these people know who I am?"

To have healthy supportive Christian community, there must
be an atmosphere where each person feels free to share authentically about what they are thinking and experiencing in their
current life situations. Out of that authenticity, people in a group
come to realize that, as Paul wrote to the church in Ephesus, we
all fall short of the glory of God. None of us is alone in that.

If people do not feel free to share authentically, it leads to
great distortion about what is really possible in life. It also causes
serious loneliness in the church. Bruce Larson said it poignantly:

The church, unfortunately, has become a museum to dis-
play the victorious life. We keep spotlighting people who
say, "I've got it made. I used to be terrible, but then I met
Jesus, got zapped by the Spirit, got into a small group, got
the gifts and fruit of the Holy Spirit..." and the implica-
tion is that they are sinners emeritus. That's just not true...

When we pretend that we once sinned, but don't now, we
produce a church where loneliness is rampant, a place where
I know I'm not making it but I assume everybody else is.[2]

A fourth reason it can be hard to get to know more than just
part of a person at church is that we really get to know people
by living some life with them. Unfortunately, many activities at
churches are not really designed for sharing lives. True, you are
there together with other people, but the interaction is mostly

talk. You don't really experience much of the life of the people around you, so your view of them is very incomplete.

We could do a lot better at creating opportunities to share life together. We need to see each other in a variety of life situations because people can be quite different from one situation to another. Camping trips are a great way to see a different side of people from what shows on Sunday mornings at church; you really do share life together. Doing service projects together also can be very helpful. For example, if you go with a team to build a house for a family in Mexico, you work and live closely with people on the team and get to know them in a far deeper and broader way than you would if you saw them only at a worship service.

Sharing Life in Supportive Community

Getting together in small groups can be a wonderful way to build a supportive community that learns to share life authentically. But there certainly is a learning curve to achieving this goal. You might first try out a small group in hope that the group will meet some of your needs. The oval in Figure 8-3 represents a person in a group. Let's suppose that person is you. The space in the oval represents all your needs (both the needs you know about and also those you are not aware of). Each pair of arrows relates to another person in the group. Initially you are drawn to supportive community by what you hope to receive from these relationships. You hope to find people who will be wonderful listeners, understanding, caring, supportive and encouraging. The incoming arrows show what you receive from the group. At first, you may not notice the uniqueness of what you receive from each

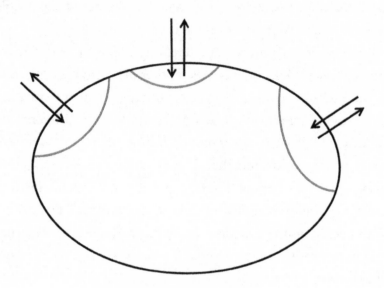

Figure 8-3. Sharing Life

person in the group, but over time you become aware of this. These individual contributions all add up to form the supportive community you experience.

A wonderful shift occurs as you begin to discover that the arrows also go out from you toward each other person in the group; you find that you can help meet the others' needs as well as having them meet yours. These developing two-way relationships with individual group members are much more satisfying (and much healthier) than one-way relationships. It feels good to realize that you have something to give to other people and that the group is not just about what you receive from it. Hopefully, the group members become able to share life with each other (not just discuss ideas) and become comfortable in sharing authentically. I like how Reggie McNeal describes the dimensions of authentic sharing:

Effective groups where people grow allow people to declare to each other what is going on in their lives, what they'd like to see going on in their lives, and what kind of help and accountability they need to move toward their hopes and away from their frustrations.[3]

Of course, in sharing our lives, we grow to see the uniqueness of each person and the value of each person's insight into our lives.

Maybe you would like to ask God to help you find or deepen supportive community in your life. If so, I'd like to invite you to pray the following prayer or one like it in your own words:

Dear God,

You know how much I long to live life as part of:

- *a community where I am known at more than a superficial level,*
- *a place where we can share each other's joys and hurts,*
- *a place where I can experience care, encouragement and accountability as I risk for your Kingdom,*
- *and a place where you can use me to help other people experience care and encouragement.*

Would you help me learn to listen to other people and enter into their lives with more of a sense of compassion?

Would you help me learn how to share the hurts and joys of my life more authentically?

God, I'm taking a few minutes to listen for what you might want to say to me about supportive community. What would you like me to hear?

CHAPTER 9

Living Out Supportive Community

No matter how many wonderful people are in the group and no matter how much we receive from (or give to) each one, there is still a large hole in the middle that can be met only by the presence and power of God in our lives and at the center of the group (see Figure 9-1). In a supportive community with God in the middle of it, we can encourage each other as we grow in our relationships with him, we can support each other as we make choices to follow his prompting in our lives and we can be there for each other when we fall short of what we wish we could be. We get the opportunity to pray for each other and to see God's answers to these prayers. We also get to see God at work growing and using other people in our group. And we have a place to share where we are growing and where God is using us.

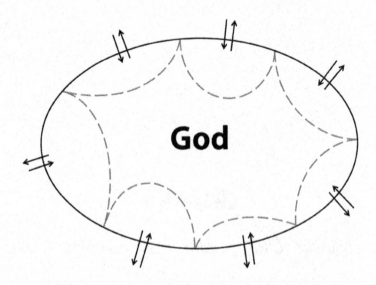

Figure 9-1. Supportive Community with God in the Middle

Bruce Larson summed up the importance of supportive community with God in our midst like this:

> *Christians, to be productive, need to be nourished, and we do this in community. We have no choice—God made us that way. Jesus said in one place, "Whatever you bind on earth will be bound in heaven, and whatever you loose on earth will be loosed in heaven." What is he talking about? What is this power to bind and loose? Well, if all of us fail and none of us are sinners emeritus, we must be forgiven—Jesus says here that my release comes at the hands of another. That is one purpose of a small group: to loose crippled people from the sins that restrict them, to call forth gifts, to set people free, to deploy them in the world.[1]*

Choosing to be part of such an authentic supportive community is an important step we can take. But this can often feel like quite a risk. Larson discussed this risk in his own experience and shared the wonderful result of making that choice:

> *God asks, "Will you entrust yourself to a part of my family, yes or no?" ... I remember God saying, "Well, Bruce, you're about average. A few people may be a bit better than you, and a few a bit worse. But the deal is this: Will you, as an act of faith in me, entrust yourself to somebody like you?" I said, "You're kidding." But eventually I said, "OK, I will." And when I did, it was like Pentecost for me. The power of God was suddenly released when I gave up being invulnerable.*[1]

Biblical Model for Christian Community

In the book of I Corinthians, Paul paints an amazing picture of what is possible due to the power and presence of the Holy Spirit in our midst.[2] We as the Church are a team of people so affected by each other that he uses the analogy of a human body to describe these close relationships. I believe Paul's words of wisdom concerning the Church are also a helpful model for groups and ministry teams within a church.

Paul tells us that each person is given a gift by the Spirit and that this gift is to be used for the common good. There are three important lessons here for a group. First, we can be certain that each of us has received at least one gift for use in ministry to other people in the group. We may not know what this gift is, but I Corinthians 12 assures us that we each have one. Second, we need to remember that this gift comes from the Holy Spirit; we are not the source. And finally, we are to use this gift for the common good; it isn't given to us for ourselves. The problem is that we can rarely see our gifts ourselves, so we need other people around us to help us discover our gifts. People who are around you and know you will usually see your gifts before you do.

According to Paul, our gifts are different from one person to another. We are members of God's Kingdom but not like members of a club, where each person has about the same function as another and can be replaced easily. Rather, we are members of God's Kingdom in the sense of being members of a body, where each member is quite different from the others and each has an important, unique role. Thus it should be no surprise that there is diversity in the Kingdom. God designed it that way. God also planned that we would work together in harmony, as one body belongs together and works together as a whole.

Paul makes two additional points that are very important for building effective Christian community. The first is that each of us Christians belongs to the body of Christ whether we feel like it or not. It is very easy to compare my abilities with the strengths of other people and, because I'm not gifted in the same ways that they are, believe I don't measure up. Then it's easy to believe I'm not needed and don't quite belong. But Paul's words remind me that the foot cannot say, "Because I am not a hand, I do not belong to the body." We all belong and our gifts are needed as part of our Christian supportive community. God designed us that way!

The second point is that all the other members of God's community belong to the Body of Christ whether we like it or not. We cannot leave out those whom God has called to the Body. This means there will be great diversity, just as God planned. So we must accept each other. Furthermore, we all need each other. As Paul said, "The eye cannot say to the hand, 'I don't need you.'" When one part of the body hurts, the whole body hurts; the hand cannot ignore the aching foot. God designed us to be interdependent; we are to work together as a whole in sympathetic relationship with one another. If one suffers, we all suffer. If one rejoices, we all rejoice.

So we really do belong to each other and need each other. God designed us that way. Together we are stronger, not just because of numbers but also because we have complementary skills, expertise, insight and vision. We grow from this composite competence; God doesn't give it all to just one person.

I like the story of the blind men who encounter an elephant. One grabs the tail and thinks of an elephant as an animal that is thin and long. Another touches its side and thinks an elephant is big and flat. Another touches a tusk and thinks of the elephant as rounded, hard, inflexible and pointed at the end. Still another touches the elephant's ear and thinks of an elephant as large, flat, thin and very flexible. None of the blind men has a picture of the complete elephant, though each person has an accurate part of the picture. The real elephant is a composite of each person's understanding. In a similar way, God gives each of us Christians a piece of his insight and vision. As we listen to each other, we grow a bigger, more complete picture of God, his Kingdom and what he is doing to bring transformation to our neighborhoods, our town or city and our world. We grow from listening to each other.

God uses different people in a group to be key in different situations and times. We take turns supporting each other, sometimes gathering around one person and sometimes around another. The roles may change, switch or rotate. Figure 9-2 illustrates this wonderfully. Neither the boy nor the girl is tall enough to use the drinking fountain, but working together they can reach it. The illustration shows the girl drinking, with the boy making it possible. But you can easily imagine that the roles will then switch, with the girl enabling the boy to drink. Christian community is like that. Together we do things that none of us can do alone. We need each other. And we are there for each other.

Photo by Jay Flaming.

Figure 9-2. Helping Each Other

Being there for each other means we help each other to know we belong. It means we know each other and help each other see the gifts that God has given each of us for the common good. It also means we care for each other and help each other when needed. In addition, it means we affirm each other and encourage each other to risk for God. It means we bring out the best in each other and, when helpful, we challenge each other. One person interviewed for the SG Project said this about the value of sharing lives and being influenced by other people in a supportive group:

> *With the people around me, I'm going to talk with them about me and I'm going to talk with them about them. Kind of iron sharpening iron.*

And another told of a supportive friendship that was valuable in challenging each other:

> *We do spur each other on, but my friend is good at challenging me. I don't think a lot of people have friends like that.*

Growing Supportive Community

Most people long for significant supportive community, but they don't always know how to get it. Ironically, we get it by *giving* supportive community. I discovered this quite by surprise. For junior high, I attended a very small school in a country outside the United States. The school was so small that the junior high and senior high students were combined, and even then we had a total of only six to eight students. Then my family moved back to Seattle, where I went to a large urban high school of about twenty-seven hundred students. Talk about culture shock! I did fine academically but really didn't know much about how to grow relationships with other students.

After high school I went to a large public university and, in the middle of that time, started attending a rather large college-age group at a nearby church. Knowing what it was like to feel unconnected, I decided to work at getting to know people, especially those who did not seem to be already connected. So, each week I wrote down the names of some people I had met and jotted down some notes to remind me what they looked like and some information that had come out of conversation with them. When I got home, I wrote the information about each person on a note card. During the following week, I reviewed each of those cards, recalling each person's name, what the person looked like and what information I had discovered from our conversation. With this process, the chances were good that if I saw these folks again the next week, I would be able to recognize them and call them by name. Over the next two years, I got to know more than four hundred students this way.

This turned out to be a great way to connect with people in the group, and in the process, I learned some important things about growing supportive community:

- Most people want to get to know other people, but many could use a little help getting started.
- It doesn't take much to start a conversation with someone you don't know. A little initiative is all that is usually needed.
- Just one person working at relationships can make a significant difference, even in a large group.
- It is possible to leverage your impact in reaching out to new people by introducing them to other people you already know.

Many conversations can be very superficial, but there are some things you can do to help conversations go deeper and move toward a more meaningful relationship. Good questions are important for growing relationships. This is not just a technique to get people to talk; it's a way to grow relationships through *listening*. Ask a broad range of questions that help explore the life of the person with whom you are talking. You might explore questions like the following (note the wide variety in depth of these questions; they wouldn't all be asked the first time you meet someone!):

- What are three fun things about [put the name of the person you are talking to here]?
- How did you happen to come to [insert the name of the town or city where you are having this conversation]?
- What are some of your favorite places in [insert the name of the town or city where you live]?
- What things gave you great delight last year?
- What do you hope happens this year?
- What are the growing edges for you as a Christian?

Another key to growing deeper relationships is sharing your life in conversations. Although discussing ideas or engaging in a spirited debate can be a lot of fun, it's the sharing of life that grows significant relationships. As you share your life in an authentic way, as you are willing to be vulnerable about who you are, it becomes more inviting for other people to share their lives with you. And, of course, when people share their lives with you, listen! Listen for what is important to them. Listen for what brings delight to them. Listen for what brings excitement to them. Listen for what causes them hurt. Listen, listen, listen! If you really listen, people will come to feel comfortable sharing almost anything with you, and this will grow relationships that are significant and deep.

In conversations, listen for the hearts of people who are talking; listen for the places of passion. I like the way Reggie McNeal expressed this:

> *When you are speaking to them, pay attention to when you see the lights come on (does it happen when you employ a certain phrase, a sentence, an idea?). When do you sense the energy go up? What causes people to lean forward in their seats a bit? These responses are clues that you are on to something.*[3]

Of central importance in growing Christian supportive community is listening for the spiritual needs and perspectives of people around you and listening for what God is doing in the life of each person. It varies greatly from one person to another.

Having a strategy for helping new people connect is a key component of growing supportive community. Small groups are one part of this strategy, but there can be other components as well. Some people are wonderful at noticing new people in a group and at taking the initiative to strike up conversations with people they don't yet know. They are also very good at introducing newcomers to other people. These actions help a new person feel welcomed and cared for and provide a starting point for growing other relationships. Some people are especially good at this host role, but anyone can do it. It's an attitude, an approach to a group. Even a small number of such people can completely change the character of a group, creating a welcoming, caring environment. Isabelle Goddard, the wife of a pastor who had an enormous impact in several churches on the West Coast, had a wonderful phrase for this attitude in a group: "Everyone a host." She kept reminding people that whatever group they are in, they can be a host.

Supportive community does not usually happen by accident. If you want to grow supportive community, it must become a priority. I know of one church in the Seattle area that places such a high priority on growing relationships between people that once a month twenty-five minutes are reserved during the worship service (after a short sermon) for people to share life in groups of eight in the context of the sermon. Unlike a typical small group, these are random groupings. Each group includes a facilitator who moderates the conversation and encourages life sharing. The facilitator has a list of questions that can be used to stimulate sharing. Having a facilitator and a list of sharing questions designed to encourage sharing of lives (rather than just discussing concepts head-to-head) provides a wonderful way for everyone to experience a significant interaction with others who are there that Sunday. Even a visitor gets the opportunity to connect in a meaningful way with seven other people.

Task-Oriented Supportive Community

It is not enough that we have a good time together, that we belong, that we are loved and cared for and supported and affirmed and encouraged. It is not even enough that our community has a faith dimension that is alive and vital and growing. We exist for more than ourselves; God has called us together in order to serve him through advancing his Kingdom. There is a task dimension to God's family. It troubles me that our churches often have wonderful fellowship opportunities with little sense of task. Often there seems to be no reason to be together other than to have a good time. To be sure, getting together should be enjoyable, but it is very shallow if that's all there is to it. When we see God at work through ourselves, through the people around us and through our church to make a difference in people's lives and in our world, it gives our community life, vitality and a sense of meaning. God intends to be at work both in us and through us. To have just fellowship without task or ministry robs life of both its meaning and its excitement.

However, we also need to be alert to an opposite problem that can occur: we can get so caught up in the task portion of a ministry that the community dimension is forgotten. Have you ever been on a church committee where there was only a task emphasis and almost no community? In such a group, people sit down, someone calls the meeting to order and an agenda is "covered." Someone there might be really hurting, but the whole meeting takes place without anyone ever knowing. Or maybe someone at the meeting has a great joy, but you don't find out about it until two weeks later. Maybe this person even sat next to you during the entire meeting. Unfortunately, experiences like these do happen.

Another frequent mistake is to misunderstand the meaning of harmony within the Christian community. A ministry team is a group not only with a unity that comes from God but with a diversity that is God-given as well. Anyone who expects a task group in the church to be all sweetness and light either does not understand people or has never been involved in a ministry group. *Apparent* total harmony can sometimes occur when only one person has vision or passion for the task. *Apparent* total harmony also sometimes occurs when nobody has strong vision or passion for the task. But genuine total harmony, when many or all members of a group are strongly committed to a task, is at best very difficult and probably impossible. It can be very painful to find that you disagree with other team members concerning a task. How do you work at handling these disagreements in a godly way? If I belong to Christ and you belong to Christ, we all belong to Christ together, but we can still see things differently. Real strength and growth in a group involved in a ministry come from a godly blending of people who all have vision and passion for the task. This is not usually a trivial process.

Fortunately, task groups in the Kingdom of God have special resources that can help them be quite different from a secular committee. Unfortunately, many do not use these resources and thus fail to be much different from a non-Christian group. Nonetheless, we do have special resources for drawing out the strengths from each person and blending them into a whole that is greater than the sum of its parts. Because of God's power in each member and in the group as a whole, and because he intends for us to relate to each other in the process of working together, task groups in the Kingdom of God can expect to come up with solutions that are better than any one person could devise—even the strongest person in the group. And because of God's power, we can work through differences in opinion or passion.

In the book of Romans, Paul gives some excellent suggestions for working at genuine harmony in the midst of our diversity.[4] We are not to look down on fellow Christians with whom we disagree or condemn them, remembering that God loves us equally. And we need to remember with humility that God does not give perfect insight to just one person; we need each other to enlarge our picture of what God sees and what is important to him. Furthermore, it is helpful to remember that we, too, will stand before God's judgment seat and that we are not perfect people either.

In his letter to the Romans, Paul also provides some suggestions for moving toward Christian unity.[5] We are to work at bearing with the failings of our Christian brothers and sisters (as well as our own). As servants of each other, we are to work at building each other up. In the process, God himself will give us a spirit of unity as we follow Christ's example of servant leadership.

These are tall orders, but God's power within us brings extra resources to help us learn and grow in these directions. We will fail others in the process, and others will fail us. But the power of God will be most strongly displayed in how we handle these failures. Through his power within us, we can confess our failings, receive forgiveness (from God and those we hurt) and discover reconciliation as brothers and sisters serving a common master.

Supportive Christian community is not just for me. It is not just for me and my family. It is not just for me, my family and my friends. God has something much bigger in mind. He plans on using us as part of his plan to transform the world. He's already implementing his plan, and he invites us to join in.

Maybe you would like to ask God to help you find or deepen supportive Christian community in your life. If so, I'd like to invite you to pray the following prayer or one like it in your own words:

Dear God,

Thank you for your remarkable plan for significant community. It's breathtaking!

I want to be part of an authentic, supportive community centered around you.

I want to learn how you've gifted me to be in a group and to use and grow these gifts to help groups I am in to grow significant community.

Help me to learn from the gifts of others in the groups I'm in and to encourage and affirm them as they use and grow their gifts.

Especially where there are disagreements, will you help me be a good listener, one who brings humility, wisdom, compassion and healing?

Will you teach me to listen to people, to listen for their heart and passion and where you are at work in them?

CHAPTER 10

Really? Me?

As you have been reading this book and thinking about spiritual growth, have you wondered how much you might need to grow before God could use you to make a difference? Have you ever wondered if God really could use you at all? Have you ever felt that you are not good enough to be used by God or that you don't know enough or that you are too much of an amateur Christian? Could God really use imperfect, amateur *you*? Maybe you have thought, "God, I can see how you could use my pastor, but *me*?" Or maybe you have thought, "God, I can see how you are using my friend Jennifer, but *me*?? I'm not good enough. I don't know enough. I haven't a clue how to make a difference for you."

In the Old Testament of the Bible, we read an account of a time the Lord spoke to Jeremiah:

> *The word of the Lord came to me, saying "Before I formed you in the womb I knew you, before you were born I set you apart; I appointed you as a prophet to the nations."[1]*

Maybe Jeremiah thought God had the wrong person. This is how he replied to God:

> *"Alas, Sovereign Lord," I said, "I do not know how to speak; I am too young."[2]*

Jeremiah did not feel adequate. How could he be a prophet when he was so young? How could he be a prophet when he did not know how to speak? Jeremiah must have thought, "A prophet for God? Seriously? Me?"

Maybe you've had thoughts like that, too: "How could God use me? I don't know enough. I'm not trained enough. I'm not experienced enough." Or, like Jeremiah, you might think, "I am too young."

But the remarkable news is that God can use us as we are. He chooses to use us even if we think (or know) we are inadequate. Those inadequacies don't stop God at all. The power to make something significant happen comes from God anyway. As one interviewee commented when talking about a period of high spiritual growth:

> *I've never been prepared for the task I was given. It was like I was told, "It doesn't matter; just show up." I knew I needed God's help.*

Yes, our part is to be available to God, to show up. When we do, God will supply what is needed to fill in where we feel inadequate. And we can be sure that while God uses us as we are, he will also be growing us.

A Leaky Hose

Maybe you've thought, "If I could just get good enough, then I could believe that God could use me. But I'm like a leaky hose; I know I have flaws. I'm just not good enough. I could see how God could use a perfect hose, but what about me?"

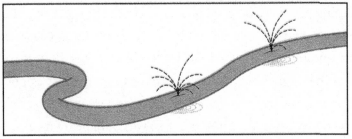

Illustration by Jon Garcia.

Figure 10-1. The Hose Leaks

The incredibly good news is that God can use even leaky hoses. We are containers that God can use to get living water through to where it is needed. We are not the water and we don't push it through. God supplies the water and God pushes it through. OK, so we are imperfect; you and I are leaky hoses. But God's plan is to use us anyway—as we are. As Paul said when he wrote to the church in Corinth:

> *For God, who said, "Let light shine out of darkness,"*
> *made his light shine in our hearts to give us the light*

of the knowledge of God's glory displayed in the face
of Christ. But we have this treasure in jars of clay to
show that this all-surpassing power is from God and
not from us.[3]

God knows that we have weaknesses and that we are imperfect. God chooses to use us anyway. That's his plan. Our flaws don't matter; they don't stop him. And while God uses us as we are, we can be sure he will also be growing us.

These Hands Have Jelly on Them

Training people to be good is not the central purpose of a church, but sometimes people talk as if it is. This thinking causes some severe problems for Christian leadership. In this view, if we are not going to mess up the act, we have to be at least as good as the people we lead. To be better than they are would be helpful. To be perfect would be best of all, so we could be living examples of a perfect life. And in this kind of church, guess what the pastors—above all, the senior pastor—have to be? They have to be perfect plus! But it just isn't possible for any of us as human beings to be perfect or to model perfection.

Sometimes this misconception is strengthened by the over-glamorizing of the heroes of the Bible. But stop to think about it. Who was called "a man after God's own heart"? It was King David, and God called him that. But David was hardly perfect; the Bible tells of some very serious mistakes he made. However, God clearly loved and used him anyway. And look at Peter. God used him to do incredible things, and he's certainly a biblical hero. But Peter suffered from quite a runaway mouth, among other faults. When we carefully read through the Bible and look at the Old Testament and New Testament heroes, it is clear that they had real flaws. Still, we see that God used those imperfect people to do incredible things to advance his Kingdom. This is a breathtaking realization.

Should we even try to be good people? Certainly! But goodness is not our main goal; it is a byproduct of walking with God. Our main goal is to be available for God to use us just as we are; this is God's expectation. Then, when we fall short of goodness, we need to admit it and say we're sorry. We can then receive God's forgiveness, cleansing and restoration.

What wonderful, encouraging news! We can dare to believe that God can use us even though we aren't perfect. It is tragic that so many Christians today have the impression that they are not good enough for God to use them, that if and when they become better people (good people), only then God could use them. But he simply invites us to be available to him. Accepting that invitation is the fundamental thrust and main purpose of Christian life, rather than being good. Then, along the way, goodness seems to grow as a byproduct of God's work through us and in us.

In the *Peanuts* comic strip in Figure 10-2, Linus is looking at his hands with fascination. He sees that they have the potential to make a significant difference in his world. But when Lucy looks closely at his hands, she discovers (and announces) that they have jelly on them. These hands that were going to change the world around him have jelly on them! Hmmm. This makes Linus wonder if those hands really could make a significant difference after all.

Figure 10-2. These Hands Have Jelly on Them

Usually we don't need someone else to point out that our
hands have jelly on them; we are very much aware of it ourselves.
I remember one evening when a friend called to tell me that her
seventh grade son, Dan, had decided not to go to school any
longer. There were only two weeks left in the school year, and she
asked if I would come over and talk to her son. I knew Dan quite
well and liked him, so I said I would be right over. Before leaving
my house, I called two friends and asked them to pray for the
conversation I would be having with Dan.

I drove to Dan's house and we talked for a while. It was
a good conversation, and I could see what the problem was.
Dan had mouthed off a bit to some other boys and was afraid
that if he went back to school, there would be problems with
those guys. He absolutely would not agree to go back to school
for those last two weeks, no matter what. I could not think of

anything else to do or say, so I got up to leave. At the door, I decided to tell Dan that I was angry that he was throwing away the end of his school year. I intended it to be a matter-of-fact authentic statement, but to my astonishment, as I spoke, a flood of anger washed over me; I really was mad. I opened the front door, walked out and slammed the door behind me. Once outside, I was mortified at my behavior; it was so clearly the wrong thing to have done. As I got into my car, I also realized I would have to tell my friends who were praying what had just happened. Of course, I did call them, but I didn't feel at all good about what I had to share. I had trusted that God would use my conversation with Dan, but now I felt like my hands had jelly all over them.

The next day I talked with Dan's mom and discovered two remarkable things. First, Dan had been so hurt when I stormed out the door that it led to a wonderful conversation with his mom in which she could just be Mom to him. Second, Dan actually did decide to go back to school that morning; I had not thought this was even a possibility.

As I shared this whole story with some friends, they marveled at the outcome and suggested that I really had done the right thing in storming out the door—look at the wonderful outcome. But I knew better; it was definitely not how I would have wanted to interact with Dan as I left. God just used even my big mistake to do something really good. My hands had jelly on them, but that did not prevent God from using me anyway.

It's amazing, but God does choose to use these hands with jelly on them. That's his plan. And while God uses us as we are, we can be sure he will also be growing us.

Where's the Fresh Edge of Paint?

Recently we repainted one of the rooms in our house. As we worked, part of the room where we had already painted was drying. The more recently painted places were not as dry. And where we just painted there was a very wet edge of paint.

Illustration by Abigail Platter.

Figure 10-3. The Fresh Edge of Paint

When God works in our lives, it's much like the room-painting project. There are places or events in our past where God's work in us is plainly evident, and we enjoy sharing those experiences with other people. There are also more recent places or events where we see that God has been at work in us. And then there are the places where God is growing or stretching us right now. This is like the fresh edge of paint.

Where is your fresh edge of paint? Where is God working right now in your life? Where is he using you right now? If there doesn't seem to be a fresh edge of paint, it's probably time to risk for God, to make yourself available to him to stretch and grow you.

The Microphone Principle

When we attempt to do things for God, we find that he more likely is doing things through us. His power shows up to use what we put in his hands to do far more than we could ever ask, plan or even imagine. Paul said it like this to the church at Ephesus:

> *Now to him who is able to do immeasurably more than all we ask or imagine, according to his power that is at work within us, to him be glory in the church and in Christ Jesus throughout all generations, for ever and ever! Amen.*[4]

Imagine that you are invited to speak to five thousand people in a large auditorium. Because there are so many people, you speak into a microphone, and the sound of your voice is amplified and sent out from large speaker enclosures. What you hear is only the simple sound of your voice, but the audience hears something different: the greatly amplified sound of your voice from the speaker enclosures.

Illustration by Abigail Platter.
Figure 10-4. Speaking to a Large Group

There's a similar effect when we risk doing something for God. He takes what we do or say and greatly magnifies what we put in his hands. Maybe this happens when we talk with someone and God uses that conversation out of all proportion to what we actually said to the person. Maybe when we speak to a group, people hear things we are pretty sure we didn't say, because God translated our words into what they needed to hear. Sometimes a small kindness we do for another person has much more impact that we could ever imagine. It's remarkable how God can use what we put in his hands to do far more than we could ever do on our own.

I love the Bible story of the young boy who brought his lunch when he joined a very large gathering of people who had come to see and hear Jesus.[5] Toward the end of the day, Jesus's disciples knew the crowd would be getting hungry and suggested he send everyone home. Instead, he told *them* to feed the crowd. The disciples were aghast; they knew they did not have food to feed all those people. When Jesus told them to go look and see what they had, they reported back that a young boy had five loaves and two fish. That's all they could come up with.

Jesus took the five loaves and two fish, thanked God for them, broke them up into pieces and told the disciples to distribute them to the crowd. Not only did this feed more than five thousand people, but twelve basketfuls were left over after everyone finished eating. There was no way that young boy could ever have guessed that his small lunch would feed all those people (and, of course, it would not have). But when put in the hands of Jesus, that small lunch was so greatly magnified that it fed thousands of people.

Some years ago I moved with my family from Seattle to the Netherlands for a twelve-month temporary work assignment. Though we were eager to step out into this new adventure, we knew it wouldn't be easy to be so far from close friends and extended family. We wondered if it would be possible in such a short time to find Christian relationships in our new city, relationships that would fill some of the void we felt as we left our church family in Seattle. We wondered if we would run into Christians in our new town who were a "live bunch." We prayed that this might happen.

On the second day in our new house in our new town, we noticed two children next door who seemed quite interested in us. The following day, the children came over to meet us, and we discovered that they spoke English (*real* English, since they had come from England). Moreover, we discovered that these children and our children would be going to the same schools. The neighbor children gave us all kinds of helpful information about the schools, and we greatly enjoyed getting to know them. Then they introduced us to their parents, who were very friendly and helpful as well. The parents told us a lot about our new town (including where to find things we needed to buy) and helped us with the process of adjusting to a new culture. They seemed to be a very nice family, and we were deeply grateful to God for providing us with such friendly neighbors in our new city.

When Saturday of our first week arrived, we wondered again what we might do for a church family. Then, to our surprise, one of the English neighbor girls (I'll call her Kate) came over to our house, knocked at our door and asked us, "Do you love Jesus?" With great delight, we replied, "Yes, we do!" So Kate invited us to go to worship with her family the next day. Through them we were introduced to a delightfully alive Dutch congregation and also to an international English-speaking fellowship that had recently begun meeting together for worship.

How grateful we were for God's wonderful answers to our prayers for growing relationships with neighbors, for friends for our kids and for a church family. And we were deeply grateful for the neighbor kids God used to bring those answers to our prayers. Kate had asked us a simple question and given us a simple invitation, but God had used her to do far more than she ever could have imagined.

A friend told me about an experience where God had used her four-year-old daughter, Emily, to answer her prayer for help and to bring his message of encouragement. The mother was feeling quite sad and low one morning. She spent some time reading her Bible and praying, but it didn't make much difference in how she felt. She went about her morning tasks while her daughter played nearby, dancing around the room and singing. Her mother didn't really pay much attention at first, but as Emily continued to dance and sing, her mom started listening to the words of the song. As she listened, she realized they were just the words she needed to hear. She went over and asked her daughter to sing the song again just for her. She knelt down and held Emily's face in her hands as the little girl sang the song again, this time just for her mother. These were the words of the song:

> *I cast all my cares upon you.*
> *I lay all of my burdens down at your feet.*
> *And anytime I don't know what to do,*
> *I will cast all my cares upon you.*[6]

Emily's mother was deeply moved; she told Emily that the song was exactly what she needed to hear right then and asked her to sing it one more time. Emily did so, and again her singing brought her mother great encouragement; it was truly God's word to her through her daughter.

Another friend was a pastor well known for sermons that had a strong impact on those who heard him preach. In the process of getting to know him in a supporting small group, he told us that he always had butterflies in his stomach when he got up to preach. At first I thought, "What? How could this be? He's such a remarkable preacher." Later I realized that he knew what I'm calling the microphone principle: he could prepare his very best, he could preach his very best, but he knew that unless the Holy Spirit took his words and did something with them, not much would happen. He deeply hoped the Holy Spirit would translate his words and connect them to the real lives of the people listening to him. People heard much more than the words of the pastor; they heard God's personal words to them.

OK, but What About Me?

"Fine," you say, "I get how God used the small boy with the five loaves and two fish. I can see how God used Kate with your family in the Netherlands. I get how God used Emily with her mom. But me? I don't see how God could be planning to use me."

Jeremiah couldn't see it either. This chapter started out telling about the time God encountered Jeremiah as a very young person and told him he was going to be God's prophet to the nations. Jeremiah's response was to point out two rather large problems: he was too young, and he didn't know how to speak.

Here is how God replied to Jeremiah's concerns:

> But the Lord said to me, "Do not say, 'I am too young.' You must go to everyone I send you to and say whatever I command you. Do not be afraid of them, for I am with you and will rescue you," declares the Lord. Then the Lord reached out his hand and touched my mouth and said to me, "I have put my words in your mouth."[7]

God knew that Jeremiah could not, by himself, pull off what God was asking him to do. But that was never God's plan. God's plan was to send Jeremiah as his representative; he would be able to do what God was asking because of God's power working through him. Just to reinforce the point, God reached out to touch Jeremiah right where he felt weakest to assure him that

God's power and plan would not be thwarted by any weakness on Jeremiah's part. God knew that his power would be more clearly shown through a young man who *knew* he couldn't succeed without God. You see, only God can do what really counts, but nonetheless he plans on working through us in the process. We are imperfect amateurs God uses to live out his breathtaking purpose. You couldn't plan or even imagine the ways God will use you, no matter how hard you try.

God's power at work within us can solve two important problems we face in being available for his use. The first is the "want to" problem. Sometimes we are not available because we just don't want to do what we think God wants us to do. That was Jonah's problem; he was determined not to go to Ninevah to preach as God asked him to do.[8] But after we get over the "want to" problem, we still can get hung up on a "how to" problem. The disciples of Jesus encountered a major "how to" problem when he asked them to feed the crowd of five thousand, as described earlier in this chapter.[9] They didn't have a clue how to feed that many people. It seemed impossible. But Jesus had the power to solve the problem, and he enabled the disciples to be part of the solution. They followed his directions, and the whole crowd was fed from a small boy's lunch of five loaves and two fish.

In Paul's letter to the church in Philippi, he wrote, "For it is God who works in you to will and to act in order to fulfill his good purpose."[10] Paul is pointing out that God can work within us both to give us the will to do what he wants us to do and to help make it happen. Through his power at work within us, God can solve both the "want to" problem and the "how to" problem. And God is able to use us in ways that defy the imagination because of his power at work within us. It's an inside job.

This is true even with the hard stuff, the tough stuff in our lives. God does not send these experiences to us, but he sure can use them (both in our lives and in the lives of those around us) to advance his Kingdom. It isn't any harder for God to use the tough stuff in life than to use the easy stuff. Sometimes in the midst of tough stuff or our failures, God can be especially powerful. Paul tells us in his second letter to the church in Corinth that, at one point, he asked God to remove some tough stuff from his life. In fact, he asked not just once but three different times. However, this was God's response:

> *But he said to me, "My grace is sufficient for you, for my power is made perfect in weakness." Therefore I will boast all the more gladly about my weaknesses, so that Christ's power may rest on me.*[11]

Even our tough stuff, our weaknesses and our failures, do not prevent God from being at work. Just as with Paul, his grace is sufficient for us, and his power is not limited by our weakness. In fact, God's power seems to be unleashed in the face of our weakness.

I really like the story in the Alpha Course[12] about a little girl playing a piano in the hallway of a hotel. She was not a very skilled piano player, and it was rather painful to hear. After a few minutes, a man came by and sat beside her. He began to play additional notes that complemented and bridged between the "plink plunk plink" notes the little girl was playing. The resulting music sounded beautiful. It turned out that the man was the girl's father and also a well-known composer. As the Alpha Course points out, God comes alongside us in a similar way in our weaknesses and failures to add his notes to our music, creating a beautiful result from what we try to do for God.[13]

Whoever you are right now reading this book (yes, *you*), God can work in you not just to help you cope with life but to do much more. He is perfectly capable not only of helping you cope but also of using you to act for his good purpose to advance his Kingdom. Isn't that amazing news? Isn't that almost too good to be true?

It's almost unbelievable that God might be able to use us as we are and that he will supply what is needed so we can do what he has in mind. But me, really? Yes, you! Really.

God has much more in mind for us than we can possibly believe or even understand. So how can we become available for what God has in mind? Here are some suggestions to consider:

- Pray—and *listen*. When praying to God, take time to listen for God's voice.
- Pray that God will help you be available to him. Tell God you want to be available and ask him to help you say yes when he prompts you to do something for him (even if you don't yet know how to do it).
- Ask your friends to pray that you will listen for God.
- Ask your friends to pray that you will listen to God when he speaks to you.
- Ask your friends to pray that you will see God at work in those around you.
- Ask your friends to pray that you will be stretched by God. We grow spiritually from being stretched beyond who we are right now.
- Ask your friends to pray that you will risk for God outside your comfort zone.

- Ask your friends what they see as the gifts God has given you. Other people will see these gifts before you do, so ask them what they see.
- Ask your friends to pray that even in tough times (maybe especially then), God will grow you spiritually.

I would also invite you to consider praying to ask God for help in being available for his use. You could use the prayer below or, if you prefer, create one like it in your own words:

> *God, it's mind-boggling to hear that you have much more in mind for me than I can possibly believe, understand or even imagine.*
>
> *God, it's pretty amazing to hear that you intend to use me to advance your Kingdom. Really? Me?*
>
> *I do want to be available for your use.*
>
> *Would you help me to better hear your voice?*
>
> *Would you help me to be more willing to risk saying yes to your prompts?*
>
> *God, I'm taking a few minutes to listen for what you might want to say to me. What would you like me to hear?*

You can be sure that God can hardly wait to start answering a prayer like this!

Appendix A: Research Process

Summary of the Research Process

The data for the Spiritual Growth Research Project (SG Project) was obtained from personal interviews that were about an hour and a half in length. All interviews were conducted in the Puget Sound area. Potential interviewees were selected from a small mainline denominational church in Seattle, a larger mainline denominational church in Seattle and a number of other churches in the Puget Sound area. Most potential subjects were selected by the interviewer because they were known to him, and some were referred to him by people he knew. The following invitation to participate in the SG Project was sent to potential interviewees via e-mail (occasionally invitations with similar content were sent via Facebook or telephone calls):

> Hi <name>,
>
> I'm in the middle of a very interesting research project to interview 300 people to determine what factors have been most influential in helping them grow spiritually. Though there is already a lot of material on this subject, I've been increasingly aware that some of the most important causes of spiritual growth are not well-identified and only some of them get considered

when thinking about helping people grow spiritually. So I decided to interview 300 people in the Seattle area to find out what really has influenced their spiritual growth.

I would be very interested in including you as one of the folks I interview. The interview takes about an hour and a half and I could meet you any time or place that might be convenient for you (with the exception of Mondays).

Interested? If so, what times might be workable for you?

- Ted

Interviews took place in a variety of locations. Many were in coffee shops, others were at a church and a number were in the homes of interviewees. Interviewees were asked to use the life graph template (shown in Figure A-1) to think about their lives from birth to present and to divide them into periods of their choice. Then they were asked to think about how much spiritual growth had occurred in each period and to draw a horizontal line for that period at a height that would indicate how much spiritual growth (or decline) they had experienced in that period. These horizontal lines for each period were then connected together by vertical lines at the period boundaries. Interviewees were then asked to label each period with a letter and create a legend at the bottom of the graph that showed the letter of each period along with a few words describing that period.

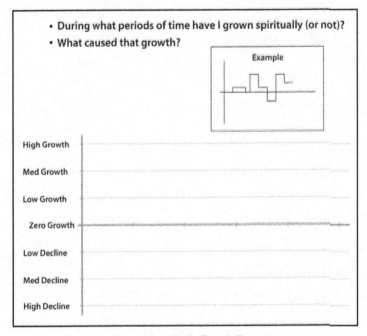

Figure A-1. Life Graph Page

Next, the interviewees were asked to look over the Spiritual Growth Causes page (see Figure A-2) and circle the appropriate impact rating for each item based on how much impact it had had on their spiritual growth.

An initial list of causes of spiritual growth was developed from a content analysis of the initial six interviews and presented to the next nine interviewees with a final line titled "Other (specify)." This captured additional causes of spiritual growth that were not on the initial printed list. The most frequently mentioned of these additional causes were added to the initial list, yielding the list shown in Figure A-2, which was used for the balance of the interviews.

	CAUSES OF MY SPIRITUAL GROWTH	IMPACT					
		None	Low		Med		High
PS	Influence by a person I looked up to	(0)	(1)	(2)	(3)	(4)	(5)
TT	Going through tough times	(0)	(1)	(2)	(3)	(4)	(5)
BK	Reading a book	(0)	(1)	(2)	(3)	(4)	(5)
RS	Taking a risk	(0)	(1)	(2)	(3)	(4)	(5)
SC	Supportive community	(0)	(1)	(2)	(3)	(4)	(5)
BI	Reading the Bible.	(0)	(1)	(2)	(3)	(4)	(5)
LD	Being in a leadership role	(0)	(1)	(2)	(3)	(4)	(5)
CL	Taking a class	(0)	(1)	(2)	(3)	(4)	(5)
CF	Going to a conference/ workshop/seminar	(0)	(1)	(2)	(3)	(4)	(5)
CG	Challenge from a person who knew me	(0)	(1)	(2)	(3)	(4)	(5)
TR	Needing to trust God because I was in over my head	(0)	(1)	(2)	(3)	(4)	(5)
MN	Being mentored	(0)	(1)	(2)	(3)	(4)	(5)
FA	Influence of family	(0)	(1)	(2)	(3)	(4)	(5)
OG	Obeying God (God's nudge/call/invitation)	(0)	(1)	(2)	(3)	(4)	(5)
AP	Seeing an answer to prayer	(0)	(1)	(2)	(3)	(4)	(5)
OT	Other (specify):	(0)	(1)	(2)	(3)	(4)	(5)

Figure A-2. Spiritual Growth Causes Page

The two-letter codes on the left side of the Spiritual Growth Causes page were used in a third part of the interview, where the interviewees were asked to look at their life graph and think about the periods of high or medium growth. Then they were asked to indicate what causes of spiritual growth applied to each of these periods. Using a two-letter abbreviation for each cause (shown in Figure A-2) took less space on the life graph than would have been required to write out the full phrase for each cause of spiritual growth. It also made the resulting life graph page less busy.

Appendix B: Summary of Interview Results

Demographics

Two hundred people were interviewed for the SG Project. These interviewees were selected because they were recommended as people who had grown spiritually in at least some part of their lives. They came from churches in the Puget Sound region in or near Seattle as shown below:

> From a small mainline denominational church: 81
> From a larger mainline denominational church: 80
> From other churches in the Puget Sound region: 39

> Total: 200

The ages of those interviewed ranged from twenty-two to eighty-nine, with the following distribution of ages:

20-29:	21	(10.5%)
30-39:	44	(22%)
40-49:	32	(16%)
50-59:	42	(21%)
60-69:	44	(22%)
70-79:	10	(5%)
80-89:	7	(3.5%)

Of those interviewed, 96 were men and 104 were women. They had the following age distribution:

	Men		Women	
20-29:	8	(8%)	13	(13%)
30-39:	18	(19%)	26	(25%)
40-49:	17	(18%)	15	(14%)
50-59:	22	(23%)	20	(19%)
60-69:	23	(24%)	21	(20%)
70-79:	5	(5%)	5	(5%)
80-89:	3	(3%)	4	(4%)
Totals:	96	(100%)	104	(100%)

Impact Ratings for the CAUSES OF MY SPIRITUAL GROWTH

Figure B-1 on the next page shows the overall results for how the interviewees rated the personal impact of various possible causes of spiritual growth shown to them during the interview (see Figure A-2).

Spiritual Growth Cause	Abbr.	Mean Rating
"Obeying God" (God's nudge/call/invitation)	OG	4.09
"Going through Tough Times"	TT	4.08
"Influence by a Person I Looked Up To"	PS	4.04
"Needing to Trust God Because I Was in over My Head"	TR	4.03
"Supportive Community"	SC	3.93
"Reading the Bible"	BI	3.70
"Being in a Leadership Role"	LD	3.54
"Seeing an Answer to Prayer"	AP	3.53
"Taking a Risk"	RS	3.47
"Influence of Family"	FA	3.07
"Challenge from a Person Who Knew Me"	CG	3.01
"Reading a Book"	BK	2.93
"Being Mentored"	MN	2.81
"Going to a Conference/Workshop/Seminar"	CF	2.53
"Taking a Class"	CL	2.47

Ratings: 0=None, 1=Low, 2=Low/Med, 3=Med, 4=Med/High, 5=High

Figure B-1. Ratings for Causes of Spiritual Growth

Five causes were rated as having the greatest impact on spiritual growth:

- "Obeying God" (God's nudge/call/invitation)
- "Going through Tough Times"
- "Influence by a Person I Looked Up To"

- "Needing to Trust God Because I Was in over My Head"
- "Supportive Community"

In general, the higher the impact rating, the greater would be its impact on spiritual growth. So if a cause has a high rating, it should be considered an effective cause of spiritual growth. The interpretation of lower ratings is more complicated. If a cause has a low rating, it could mean that it is a less effective cause of spiritual growth, but it could also mean a person hasn't had much experience with this cause. In the SG Project interviews, there was some evidence that some of the interviewees had not experienced the following causes of spiritual growth, and this could have pulled down the impact ratings for these causes:

- "Being Mentored"
- "Challenge from a Person Who Knew Me"
- "Being in a Leadership Role"

Additional observations related to the ratings for causes of spiritual growth:

- The ratings for "Obeying God" (OG) were not as much about "keeping the rules" as making the hard choices in life to actually do what people heard God inviting them to do. See Chapter 6 for more on this topic.
- For more discussion about "Tough Times" (TT), see Chapter 2.
- "Influence by a Person I Looked Up To" (PS) covered a variety of roles, including a friend, a family member,

a pastor, a missionary, a teacher, a fellow student and a boss.

- For more discussion about "Needing to Trust God Because I Was in over My Head" (TR), see Chapter 3.
- For "Supportive Community" (SC), see Chapters 8 and 9.
- Judging from the ratings for "Taking a Risk" (RS), it would appear that many people are not being stretched enough for the Kingdom (stretched enough that people need to trust God for what they are attempting to risk to do). See Chapter 7 for more about "Taking a Risk."
- "Influence of Family" (FA) took a number of different forms depending on when in life it occurred. Sometimes interviewees commented on their family of origin, sometimes they talked about their spouses, sometimes they shared the impact of their children and sometimes they talked about relatives (particularly grandparents).
- "Taking a Class" (CL) was seen as helpful for gathering information even though it may not have caused spiritual growth.

Distribution of Impact Ratings for CAUSES OF MY SPIRITUAL GROWTH

Figure B-2 shows more detail about the ratings for causes of spiritual growth, including the distribution of ratings. Note that the abbreviations in Figure B-2 are the same two-letter codes explained in Figure B-1.

Note that every cause had at least some people who rated it as having high impact on their spiritual growth (even the causes with lower overall impact ratings). Conversely, every cause had at least some people who rated the cause as having no or low impact on their spiritual growth (even the causes with overall high impact ratings).

Spiritual Growth Cause	Mean Rating	Distribution of Ratings							
		5	4	3	2	1	0	Total 5s + 4s	Total 1s + 2s
OG	4.09	86	64	35	11	4	0	150	4
TT	4.08	114	36	25	7	13	5	150	18
PS	4.04	94	49	37	12	6	2	143	8
TR	4.03	98	50	30	8	10	4	148	14
SC	3.93	71	73	38	8	9	1	144	10
BI	3.70	64	52	54	20	9	1	116	10
LD	3.54	53	58	53	18	15	3	111	18
AP	3.53	64	41	52	25	15	3	105	18
RS	3.47	54	59	42	25	12	8	113	20
FA	3.07	31	48	59	33	23	6	79	29
CG	3.01	37	49	42	34	26	12	86	38
BK	2.93	26	42	64	34	27	7	68	34
MN	2.81	32	50	37	30	31	20	82	51
CF	2.53	14	37	56	40	39	14	51	53
CL	2.47	16	29	52	52	38	13	45	51

Ratings: 0=None, 1=Low, 2=Low/Med, 3=Med, 4=Med/High, 5=High

Figure B-2. Distribution of Ratings for Causes of Spiritual Growth

In general, the distribution of ratings is not significantly bimodal. So the mean impact ratings are representative of the impact for each cause of spiritual growth. Note that "Tough Times" (TT) has by far the highest number of people who rated it as having the highest impact on their spiritual growth. However, the mean rating for "Tough Times" was not quite at the top of the causes because a significant number of other people rated tough times as having a low impact on their spiritual growth. A similar mild effect shows up for two other causes. "Challenge from a Person Who Knew Me" (CG) and "Being Mentored" (MN) have a rather higher number of people who rated these causes with a 4 or a 5 than other causes with similar overall mean ratings. This is due to the fact that a relatively larger number of other people rated these causes as having no impact. It is possible that these ratings of no impact were from people who had never experienced challenges from people who knew them or never experienced being mentored.

A second way to look at the importance of the causes of spiritual growth is to evaluate how often each of them is present in periods of medium growth or higher. Figure B-3 again shows each of the causes of spiritual growth in the order of rated impact. Note that the abbreviations are again the same two-letter codes explained in Figure B-1. But added to the column of impact ratings is a column showing how many times across all two hundred people interviewed each cause was mentioned as contributing to a period of medium or higher spiritual growth. The number of total mentions was divided by two hundred to get the mean number of mentions per person. This column gives a measure of the frequency of contribution for each of the causes.

Spiritual Growth Cause	Mean Rating	Total Mentions	Total Mentions Per Person
OG	4.09	293	1.47
TT	4.08	243	1.22
PS	4.04	298	1.49
TR	4.03	266	1.33
SC	3.93	398	1.99
BI	3.70	340	1.70
LD	3.54	256	1.28
AP	3.53	191	0.96
RS	3.47	219	1.10
FA	3.07	156	0.78
CG	3.01	144	0.72
BK	2.93	159	0.80
MN	2.81	171	0.86
CF	2.53	119	0.60
CL	2.47	118	0.59

Ratings: 0=None, 1=Low, 2=Low/Med,
3=Med, 4=Med/High, 5=High

Figure B-3. Frequency of Causes in High- to Medium-Growth Periods

To show the relationship between mean impact ratings and mean frequency counts, these values for each cause of spiritual growth are shown in graphical form in Figure B-4.

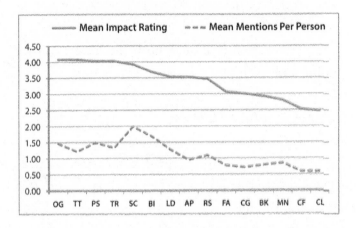

Figure B-4. Comparing Frequency with Impact of Causes

From Figure B-3 and its graphical representation in Figure B-4, you can extract the following insights about the causes of spiritual growth:

- "Supportive Community" (SC) stands out with the highest frequency of occurrence in periods of significant spiritual growth. But for impact ratings, it shared the top spot with five other causes.
- "Reading the Bible" (BI) also stands out with its second-highest frequency of occurrence in periods of significant spiritual growth. But for impact ratings, it was only sixth from the top.
- "Going through Tough Times" (TT) had a somewhat lower frequency of occurrence than might be predicted from its position in the impact-rating curve.

- Apart from the anomalies noted above, the frequency of a cause roughly tracked its rating for impact on spiritual growth, so the causes with the lower ratings also tended to have the lower frequencies of occurrence.
- "Taking a Class" (CL) had both the lowest impact rating and the lowest frequency of mention.

Other Causes of Spiritual Growth

During the rating of spiritual growth causes, interviewees were invited to add any other causes of their spiritual growth that were not already on the Spiritual Growth Causes page. Many of the additional causes were brought up by only one person, and some simply provided additional color about the causes already on the page. But some additional causes were brought up by multiple people. These causes were not necessarily described with exactly the same words, but the most common words for each group of similar ideas (and the number of mentions for each) are summarized below:

Cause	Number of People
Mission Trip	12
Holy Spirit	11
Service	10
Worship	8
Sermon	8
Seeing God at Work	5
Music	3

Examples of Completed Life Graphs

The life graphs obtained from those interviewed for the SG Project showed a remarkable variety of shapes. They showed high as well as low or declining spiritual growth at a wide variety of periods in life. With so much variety, it is not possible to show a typical graph. Instead, the five graphs shown below have been selected to illustrate the wide variety of life graphs obtained as a result of the SG Project.

The two-letter codes indicated for each high- and medium-growth period on the life graphs show what spiritual growth causes were most important in each of these periods. Note that these are the same two-letter codes explained in Figure B-1 of this appendix.

Example 1 is from a twenty-eight-year-old interviewee. This life graph is an example of one that was quite detailed (with a number of short periods of life). This person showed some spiritual growth from ages five to fifteen, lots of up and down swings from ages fifteen to twenty and mostly increasing growth rates from twenty to twenty-eight. Note the "Other" cause of spiritual growth labeled OT1 (counseling) in period K.

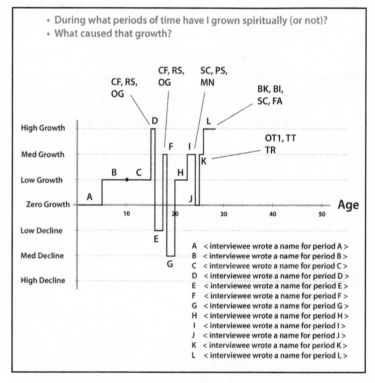

Figure B-5. Example 1 of a Completed Life Graph

Example 2 shows a life graph from someone who was thirty-eight years old. This graph shows a more typical amount of detail. Note the multiple periods of high or medium growth. This person had increasing spiritual growth rates from ages seven to fifteen, generally high growth from fifteen to twenty-five, decline in growth from twenty-five to thirty, high growth again from thirty to thirty-three and low or no growth for thirty-three and above. Note the "Other" cause of growth (direct contact with God) in period F.

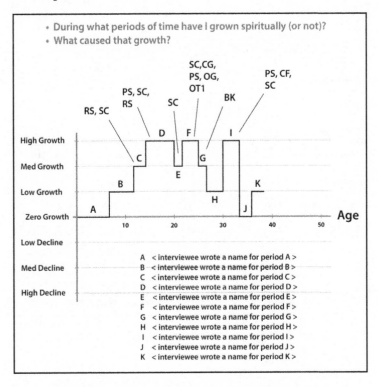

Figure B-6. Example 2 of a Completed Life Graph

Example 3, a life graph from a forty-one-year-old, shows a typical amount of detail. Note just one period of high growth and just one period of medium growth. This person had increasing spiritual growth rates from ages seven to twenty, high growth from nineteen to twenty-two and a strong decline in growth after age twenty-two.

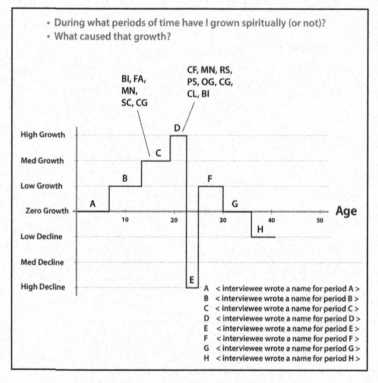

Figure B-7. Example 3 of a Completed Life Graph

Example 4, from a fifty-three-year-old, also shows a typical amount of detail. This person had increasing spiritual growth rates from ages nine to fifteen, lots of high growth from fifteen to thirty-two and then steep decline followed by increasing growth for age thirty-five and above. The life graph for this person is similar to the growth pattern of Examples 2 and 3 for ages up to twenty but quite different after twenty.

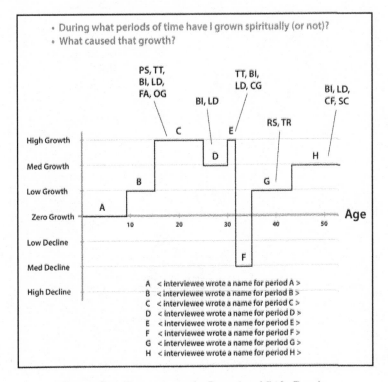

Figure B-8. Example 4 of a Completed Life Graph

Example 5 shows a life graph from someone who was eighty years old. This graph also shows a typical amount of detail. Note that this person had the strongest growth in the senior-citizen periods of life. There was really no growth before age thirty and increasing rates of growth after thirty. Note the "Other" cause of growth labeled OT1 (reflection & pondering my life experience) in period J.

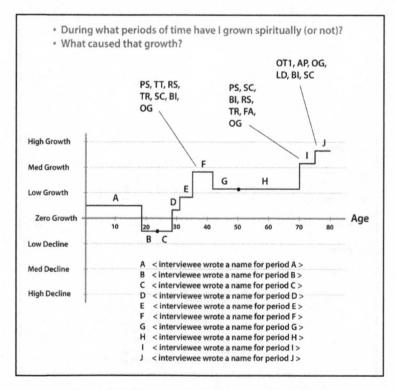

Figure B-9. Example 5 of a Completed Life Graph

Notes

Chapter 1: Are You Related to God?

1. Romans 3:23, NIV.
2. Larson, Bruce, "None of Us Are Sinner Emeritus," *Leadership Journal*, October 1, 1984.
3. Ephesians 2:8-9, NIV.

Chapter 2: Tough Times

1. Romans 8:28, NIV.
2. Maxwell, Louise, and Lisa Brihagen, "Hospital Highlight: No Chemo, No Cancer, No Kidding," *Children's Hospitals Today*, Fall 2011. www.childrenshospitals.net.
3. Genesis 50:18-21, NIV.
4. Acts 8:1.
5. Luke 15.
6. Romans 5:3-5, NRSV.

Chapter 3: Trusting God

1. II Corinthians 1:8-9, NIV.
2. Larson, Bruce, "None of Us Are Sinner Emeritus," *Leadership Journal*, October 1, 1984.
3. Luke 5:1-11.
4. Matthew 14:27-33, NIV.
5. Ruth 1.
6. Ruth 1:16, NIV.

7. II Corinthians 12:7-10.

8. Powers, Barbara, *The Henrietta Mears Story* (Ada, Mich.: Revell, 1957), 7.

9. Palmer, Earl, *Trusting God* (Vancouver, B.C.: Regent College Publishing, 2006), 27.

Chapter 4: Listening to God

1. Luke 1:26-38.

2. Luke 5:1-11.

3. John 4:4-42.

4. John 5:1-8.

5. Luke 24:32, NIV.

6. Hybels, Bill, *The Power of a Whisper* (Grand Rapids, Mich.: Zondervan, 2010), 17. Copyright © 2010 by Bill Hybels. Used by permission of Zondervan.

Chapter 5: Listening for God

1. For a thorough description of *Lectio Divina*, see Benner, David, *Opening to God: Lectio Divina and Life as Prayer* (Downers Grove, Ill.: Intervarsity Press, 2010), Chapter 3.

2. I Samuel 3.

3. See the Spiritual Direction Program description on the CFDM Northwest website at www.cfdmnorthwest.org (click on "Spiritual Direction Program").

4. Acts 10.

5. Acts 9:1-4.

6. Mark 4:1-9.

Chapter 6: Obeying God

1. Genesis 12.
2. The source for these words is unclear. Some attribute the quotation to Thomas Carlyle, a Scottish philosopher and essayist who lived from 1795 to 1881 (see Goodreads.com and Thinkexist.com), but they do not identify a source document. Others suggest various people who lived in the twentieth century as possible sources of the quotation.
3. Exodus 3-14.
4. Isaiah 55:8-9, NIV.
5. Numbers 13 and 14.
6. II Kings 5.
7. Judges 7.
8. Mark 10:14-15, NIV.
9. John 3:4, NIV.
10. John 9:1-9.
11. Larson, Bruce, *No Longer Strangers* (Word Books, 1971), 70.
12. Luke 22:47-62.
13. John 21.

Chapter 7: Getting Stretched

1. Tournier, Paul, *The Adventure of Living* (New York: Harper & Row, 1965), 117.
2. Matthew 9:9-13.
3. Acts 9.
4. II Thessalonians 1:11, NIV.

5. Larson, Bruce, "None of Us Are Sinner Emeritus," *Leadership Journal*, October 1, 1984.

6. Colossians 3:23, NIV.

Chapter 8: Supportive Community

1. McNeal, Reggie, *The Present Future* (Hoboken, N.J.: John Wiley & Sons, 2003), 137.

2. Larson, Bruce, "None of Us Are Sinner Emeritus," *Leadership Journal*, October 1, 1984.

3. McNeal, *The Present Future*, 86.

Chapter 9: Living Out Supportive Community

1. Larson, Bruce, "None of Us Are Sinner Emeritus," *Leadership Journal*, October 1, 1984.

2. I Corinthians 12.

3. McNeal, Reggie, *The Present Future* (Hoboken, N.J.: John Wiley & Sons, 2003), 100.

4. Romans 14:2-13.

5. Romans 15:1-7.

Chapter 10: Really? Me?

1. Jeremiah 1:4-5, NIV.

2. Jeremiah 1:6, NIV.

3. II Corinthians 4:6-7, NIV.

4. Ephesians 3:20, NIV.

5. Mark 6:30-44 and John 6:1-13.

6. These words are included as the "Cares Chorus" in the 1985 *Kid's Praise! 5* album from Maranatha!

Music. Copyright © 1978 Universal Music –
Brentwood Benson Publ. (ASCAP) (adm. at
CapitolCMGPublishing.com) All rights reserved.
Used by permission.

7. Jeremiah 1:7-9, NIV.

8. Jonah 1:1-3.

9. Mark 6:30-44 and John 6:1-13.

10. Philippians 2:13, NIV.

11. II Corinthians 12:9, NIV.

12. The Alpha Course is a wonderful way to introduce
non-Christians to what following Jesus is all about.
Alpha was developed at Holy Trinity Brompton,
an Anglican church in the center of London, and
is now used in many other denominations. More
than twenty-two million people have attended
Alpha. It has been presented in more than 160
countries, and Alpha resources have been translated
into more than 110 languages. More information
about Alpha can be found at www.alphausa.org or
www.alpha.org.

13. Gumbel, Nicky, *Questions of Life* (Naperville, Ill.:
Alpha North America, 2003), 111.

ABOUT THE AUTHOR

Ted Thwing was born in Seattle and has been a part of church congregations on four continents. He has served on leadership teams in children's ministries, youth ministry, college ministry, post-college singles ministry and pastoral care ministries as well as core leadership teams both for a large church and for several smaller ones. He and his wife are currently involved in a young church in a rapidly growing area of Seattle, blocks from the world headquarters of Amazon and a number of significant technology and biomedical organizations.